# Pathways to peace

# peace

Facing the future with faith
—Meditations from Isaiah 40

## John Kitchen

DayOne

Unless otherwise indicated, all Scripture quotations are from The Holy Bible, English Standard Version® (esv®), copyright © 2001 by Crossway, a publishing ministry of Good News Publishers. Used by permission. All rights reserved.

Other versions used:
Scriptures marked nasb are from the New American Standard Bible®, 1960, 1962, 1963, 1968, 1971, 1972, 1973, 1975, 1977, 1995 by The Lockman Foundation. Used by permission. (www.Lockman.org)

Scriptures marked niv are from the New International Version® (NIV) Copyright © 1973, 1978, 1984 by International Bible Society. Used by permission of Zondervan Publishing House. All rights reserved.

Scriptures marked nlt are from the New Living Translation, copyright 1996. Used by permission of Tyndale House Publishers, Inc., Wheaton, Illinois 60189. All rights reserved.

British Library Cataloguing in Publication Data available

ISBN978-1-84625-212-9

Published by Day One Publications
Ryelands Road, Leominster, HR6 8NZ

☎ 01568 613 740
FAX: 01568 611 473
email—sales@dayone.co.uk
web site—www.dayone.co.uk
North American e-mail—usasales@dayone.co.uk
North American web site—www.dayonebookstore.com

Designed by Wayne McMaster and printed by Thomson Litho, East Kilbride

Dedicated to

Julie

I thank God for the privilege of sharing with you ...

the memories of yesterday,

the blessings of today,

the possibilities of tomorrow

# Endorsements

*John Kitchen's book on Isaiah 40 is a joy to read, with its strong encouragement on how the preeminence and presence of our Lord affect all we do, think, and hope for as believers. I strongly encourage a wide usage of this book among all who need a spiritual uplift in these troubling days.*

**Walter C. Kaiser, Jr., President Emeritus, Gordon-Conwell Theological Seminary, USA**

*This is a refreshing and health-giving meditation on the grandest of all themes: the nature of God and how it affects our living today. It will strengthen your spiritual muscles and equip you to face the challenges you encounter victoriously.*

**Ajith Fernando, National Director, Youth for Christ, Sri Lanka**

*In a day and age when so many Christian books use the Word of God flippantly, John Kitchen gives us a careful and thoughtful exposition of the Scripture. Very readable while thoroughly biblical, John's writings will encourage and strengthen your heart. No matter where we are on our spiritual journey, we could all benefit from a new glimpse of God.* Pathways to Peace *gives us such a glimpse. May God use these pages to expand your view of who he is.*

**John Stumbo, former Vice-President of the Christian and Missionary Alliance and Pastor, Salem Alliance Church, Salem, Oregon, USA**

# Contents

# Preface

*You keep him in perfect peace whose mind is stayed on you, because he trusts in you.*

### Isaiah 26:3

MRIs, CT scans, X-rays—they are not purveyors of hope. They exist only to verify whether something has gone wrong. They incite worry. They call tomorrow into question. The dark, slithery fingers of their elongating shadow encircle your heart as hope disappears behind the horizon of tomorrow's "what if"s. The notations in your calendar once ruled your plans, now they tremble in anticipation of being trumped by a doctor's call. A collective breath is drawn and refuses to be released until the phone rings with the news.

A final, angry shout. A door slammed. Windows rattle in their casings. Silence. As raucous as the arguments had become, the silence—the screaming absence of his voice—is more torturous. Will he return? Is it over? What do I tell the children?

A tiny, lifeless body. A raw, winter wind whistles through a silent cemetery. A final goodbye whispered through a flower-draped casket. Gray. Hopeless. Empty. Numb. One foot willed forward in front of the other without emotion. Tear ducts drained so empty they ache. Blank stares out a window as silence envelops the limousine.

A million events assault the word "tomorrow" to make it the most uncertain word in the English language. The only thing worse than getting out of bed to face a new day is continuing to lie there feeling as you do. What now? Hope—do I even believe it exists? Or dare let my heart be vulnerable enough to grasp after it?

The sighs of this age's prophets begin to resonate in our hearts more than the words of God. "More than any other time in history," says Woody Allen, "mankind faces a crossroads. One path leads to despair and utter hopelessness. The other, to total extinction. Let us pray we have the wisdom to choose correctly."[1] Our fear is that Lily Tomlin is correct when, in the film *The Search for Signs of Intelligent Life in the Universe*, she says, "We're all in this alone."

Are we? The evidence sometimes seems to scream it's true.

There was a time when the people of God believed it was so. They were not atheists, but they were hopeless. It was not that there was no God, but that he had left them behind.

For two centuries the people of Judah had watched the decline of the northern ten tribes of Israel. Behind bolted doors and through drawn shutters, Isaiah and his contemporaries watched in horror as the ruthless Assyrian armies took their brothers to the north into exile. The Assyrians were not simply Gentiles; they were notorious for their bloody brutality. Defeating and subjugating an enemy was not enough. They were known to cut the noses, ears, and tongues from their captives, gouge out their eyes, sever their hands and feet, and then flay the skin from their bodies.

The worst nightmare of Isaiah's people had moved in across

the street and was now on the front step knocking at their door. There was no ignoring their incessant rapping.

In the midst of its sixty-six chapters of prophecy, Isaiah's book breaks for a brief historical interlude in which we are told something of these horrors (Isa. 36–39). Having crushed the ten tribes of Israel, Assyrian armies laid siege to Jerusalem (ch. 36). Hezekiah, at Isaiah's encouragement, placed his sole hope upon the deliverance of God (37:1–35). He banked everything upon the hope that God was not as absent and disinterested as it might have seemed. The result was what must go down as the greatest military miracle of human history: "And the angel of the LORD went out and struck down a hundred and eighty-five thousand in the camp of the Assyrians. And when people arose early in the morning, behold, these were all dead bodies" (37:36).

God was not distant. He did care!

But amid the jubilation a discordant note sounds. The second two chapters of Isaiah's historical interlude detail Hezekiah's capitulation to the new bully on the block— Babylon (chs 38–39). She would make Assyria look like a pigtailed, freckle-faced schoolgirl. Hezekiah trusted God and saw his powerful faithfulness (chs 36–37). Yet now he is pictured as trusting in man (chs 38–39)! First we meet the king acting in the fear of God, but now we observe him walking in the fear of man.

Isaiah watched the window of opportunity close for the ten tribes of Israel. For a brief moment, hope had shaken off the fetters of faithlessness and begun to take flight, only to be grounded again before the threats of an even worse tyrant.

These four chapters divide the book of Isaiah in half. The first thirty-nine chapters speak of judgment from God for the infidelity of his people. The last twenty-seven speak of a hopeful day of restoration for the truly repentant.

As we stand at the threshold between a fretful past and a hopeful future, what guarantee is there that tomorrow will be better than yesterday? The answer is written upon the door that is ready to swing open on the hinges of these historical chapters. Take your eyes off yesterday's judgments and turn to look at the door that is poised to swing open before you. That door is Isaiah 40. What is written upon it? What hope does it hold for tomorrow?

Someone has called the last half of Isaiah (chs 40–66) a survival guide for an uncertain future. What lies behind is dark and frightening (chs 1–39). What lies ahead is full of light and hope (chs 40–66). Which will be your experience?

Lift your hand, place it on the door, and swing it open to find out. Isaiah 40 is the first chapter of the rest of your life—should you choose to step over the threshold and enter in.

## Reflect on these points

1. *What is it that appears to threaten your tomorrow?*

2. *Why is it that our best days sometimes turn into our darkest moments?*

3. *It is in our darkest moments that God is most likely to*

*shine through with fresh hope. What makes that seem difficult to embrace right now?*

4. *The choice is yours to pursue hope. God invites you, but he will not force you.*

# The preeminence
## of God

*Get you up to a high mountain, O Zion, herald of good news; lift up your voice with strength, O Jerusalem, herald of good news; lift it up, fear not; say to the cities of Judah, "Behold your God!"*

**Isaiah 40:9**

Good! I see that you have chosen hope. Or at least you have chosen to explore its possibilities.

If Isaiah 40–66 is a survival guide to an uncertain future, what does that make chapter 40? The first chapter, of course! This is the first step toward a brighter tomorrow. What, then, is the essence of this first chapter—which then must become the essence of hope itself? That answer is found just a few lines in. It is set before us in a simple, clear command: "Behold your God!" (v. 9).

The emphatic interjection demands our attention: "Look!" "See!" We are to set our eyes upon something which up to this point has been missing from our perception of our lives and circumstances. In this case, that something is God himself.

No other action has more potential and power to inject hope than getting our estimation of God corrected, accurate, and clear. A low view of God is the essence of idolatry. A low view of God dissipates faith and incites fear. Our view of God determines the direction and outcome of life. There is no more important command issued from heaven to mankind than this.

Twice in this verse we are told to lift our voices and herald good news. What is our message? The good news is God himself. It is the welcome message that a fresh perception of who God is and what he is doing will surprise, revive, and refresh your heart.

Remove any obstacle to this command ("Get you up to a high mountain"), hold nothing back in issuing it ("lift up your voice with strength"), assert it with full confidence and authority ("herald"), shake off any reticence ("fear not")—for no single activity has more potential and power to change the direction of your life than a fresh, accurate view of who God is and what he is doing.

Our goal is God. He is the fixed point upon which we are to set the gaze of our souls. A. W. Tozer was correct: "What comes into our minds when we think about God is the most important thing about us … the most portentous fact about any man is not what he at a given time may say or do, but what he in his deep heart conceives God to be like."[1]

Our calling is to get God squarely fixed in our soul's sights and then to call his people to behold the beauty, majesty, and glory of the Lord along with us. In this, said Isaiah, Jerusalem (or Zion) is to lead the charge. There must be some who have dwelt in the holy of holies who can testify to the rest of those who name God's Name ("the cities of Judah") that God is far more wonderful than they have imagined. There is no single need of God's people in any age or in any circumstance that is greater than the need for a renewed vision of God in his glory.

Our goal is to live now in light of what eternity will reveal as reality. "It will be said on that day, 'Behold, this is our God; we have waited for him, that he might save us. This is the LORD; we have waited for him; let us be glad and rejoice in his salvation'" (Isa. 25:9).

When we understand the structure of Isaiah's prophecy we are more likely to appreciate the strategic nature of this key command. Isaiah contains sixty-six chapters. The Bible itself is comprised of sixty-six books. A coincidence? Perhaps, but hold the two together again and look further at their similarities. The Old Testament contains thirty-nine books, the New Testament twenty-seven. Similarly, the book of Isaiah is comprised of two parts: The first thirty-nine chapters set forth the just judgment of God against sin. The last twenty-seven chapters (40–66) comprise the good news of a coming Redeemer who will save his people from their sins. This second half of Isaiah begins with a prophecy (40:3–5) later fulfilled in the ministry of John the Baptist (Matt. 3:3; Mark 1:3; Luke 3:4–6; John 1:23), who opened the way for Jesus's ministry. The book of Isaiah ends with a revelation of the new heaven and new earth which will bring to a climax the redemptive work of God (chs 65–66), just as the New Testament closes with the same vision (Rev. 21–22).[2] Four hundred years of silence from God were sandwiched between the Old and New Testaments. It was a time of divine testing. It was a period of terror for those waiting upon God. Isaiah 40 is thus a word for when God seems silent. When God seems distant, uninterested, detached, and uninvolved, he tells you that the greatest single thing you can do is "Behold your God!"

A fresh vision of God in his glory is what Isaiah 40 provides for us. And what do we find when we take a look? A simple proposition: *Only God's presence sustains you in the panic of an uncertain future, and God's presence only brings you peace when you appreciate his preeminence over all things.*

Read it again—it is the path of life. Isaiah 40 leaves two great wonders of God lingering before our mind's eye: his preeminence and his presence. The latter only means anything in view of the former. It is, therefore, with his preeminence that we must begin. God's preeminence forms the core of this chapter (vv. 12–26) and around it is packed the hopeful good news of his presence (vv. 1–11; 27–31).

If you wonder why God has felt so far away, examine the thoughts you have been thinking of him. The *fact* of his presence is constant. The *sense* of his presence is released only in the heart that has preoccupied itself with his preeminence. As J. Elder Cumming has well said, "In almost every case the beginning of new blessing is a new revelation of the character of God—more beautiful, more wonderful, more precious."[3] God makes himself at home in the heart that has prepared for its most honored Guest.

Take heart! A deeper, fuller, more intimate encounter with God awaits you. When you set your heart on magnifying God's greatness, you open the door to a whole new level of relationship with him (Rev. 3:20).

God is calling to you. Answer the door. Come, enter in.

## Reflect on these points

*1.* *Nothing has the potential to arouse hope like a fresh perception of who God truly is. In what way may your discouragement and darkness be linked to a misperception of God's character and nature?*

*2.* *Our goal at present is to live in the light of what eternity will reveal reality to have been. To what angle of reality might you be currently blinded?*

*3.* *When God seems far removed, look again. Take time to be still in God's presence. Recount again—by faith—the truth of his attributes. Affirm the facts of his essential character.*

*4.* *The fact of God's presence is constant. The sense of his presence is released only in the heart preoccupied with his glory.*

# The preeminence
# of God over
# all the earth

*Who has measured the waters in the hollow of his hand and marked off the heavens with a span, enclosed the dust of the earth in a measure and weighed the mountains in scales and the hills in a balance?*

*Who has measured the Spirit of the LORD, or what man shows him his counsel?*

*Whom did he consult, and who made him understand? Who taught him the path of justice, and taught him knowledge, and showed him the way of understanding?*

### *Isaiah 40:12–14*

Life is about perspective. It's about seeing things as they really are, not as they may appear through the lenses ground into shape by our anxieties. Reality is that God is preeminent. In order to impart this perspective Isaiah puts to us a series of questions.

"Who has measured the waters in the hollow of his hand?" Few things in creation seem as overwhelming as the volume of the oceans' waters. The oceans cover 71 percent of the earth's surface—140 million square miles. In total volume the earth is covered by 322,300,000 cubic miles of water. The water pressure at the deepest point of the ocean is more than eight tons per square inch—the equivalent of stacking fifty jumbo jets upon your chest. How unthinkable that someone could measure the vast store of the oceans, seas, lakes, and rivers in the hollow of one hand!

Perspective.

Or, asks Isaiah, who has "marked off the heavens with a

span?" The Milky Way—our stellar address—is approximately 100,000 light-years in diameter. Perspective requires that we remember that light travels at 186,000 miles per second. You would have to travel nonstop (no refueling, supper, or potty breaks included) for 100,000 years at that rate of speed just to reach the far side of our galaxy. Think that is undoable? Plan a trip to one of our near neighbors, the Andromeda Galaxy. It's a mere 2.3 million light-years distant from us. And what of the vast, unsearchable reaches of dark space beyond?

Lift up your eyes and look about—God measured out all of this "with a span." The "span" was a standard unit of measure in the Hebrew world. It was the distance from the tip of the thumb to the tip of the pinky finger when a hand was spread. If you lift your hand and draw it up to your face, you can obscure the entire sky. But that is mere sleight of hand. God measures off the seemingly infinite reaches of space with his hand. What would require miracle speeds and multiple lifetimes for us to span, God measures off with a hand's breadth.

Perspective.

Who "enclosed the dust of the earth in a measure and weighed the mountains in scales and the hills in a balance?" Two scientists from the University of Washington have determined that the earth weighs 5.972 sextillion tons or, in layman's terms, 5,972,000,000,000,000,000,000 metric tons.[1] Who can take all of that, pour it into a measuring cup, run a flat edge across the top, and declare its measure? Who can dump it in a Tupperware pot and then "burp" the lid to keep it fresh?

Who can take all 29,028 feet of Mt. Everest—not to mention all the other peaks of the world—and maneuver them onto a scale? Our friends from the University of Washington are only taking a scientific guess at the earth's weight. God knows.

Perspective!

All four of these metaphors attempt to describe the indescribable greatness of God. All four represent that which is completely beyond mankind, yet is within the recourse of God. Please understand, these are not hyperbolic statements (exaggerations to make a point). These are actually understatements. For if God is indeed infinite, as he claims to be, then he is greater even than these unimaginable comparisons. These are, in fact, puny comparisons from God's side, though colossal and incalculable from ours.

Having overawed us with God, Isaiah dares ask another series of perspective-giving questions:

> Who has directed the Spirit of the LORD,
> Or as His counselor has informed Him?
> With whom did He consult and who gave Him understanding?
> And who taught Him in the path of justice and taught Him knowledge
> And informed Him of the way of understanding?
>
> (NASB)

Isaiah's first questions revolved around the physical world, a place we are somewhat familiar with. They were designed to dwarf us before God on what we consider to be our own turf. These latter questions pertain to the spiritual world—a realm we are not so familiar with—and are similarly designed to bring us to our knees.

This is important because the spiritual world is where the heart of our anxieties resides. The first questions (about the physical universe) were asked merely to prepare us to accept the magnitude of God over this realm (the spiritual universe). Isaiah overwhelms us with God's preeminence in the one so that he can overwhelm us with God's preeminence over the other. This is because most of our anxiety-laced questions begin not with "what" and "where," but "why" and "whom."

Life is overwhelming. Life is meant to be overwhelming. The choice of living a doable life or being overwhelmed by life is not an option put before us. Ours is simply the choice to decide what will overwhelm us. Will we be overwhelmed by distortions of reality related to the size and magnitude of the challenges before us? Or will we be overwhelmed in worship before the God who governs and engulfs these challenges in the magnitude of his own Person?

Perspective.

Isaiah's disquieting question marks will soon enough give way to the safer ground of periods. Queries pave the way for declarations. But, before we move on, let the questions have their designed effect.

Are you in a position to counsel God about his administration of the universe and your part in it? Has he ever come up against the far wall of his knowledge and found it necessary to turn to you for assistance? Is he befuddled and left wondering what his next move should be? Isaiah's compatriots thought God unjust (v. 27). Their circumstances goaded them into assuming their righteousness surpassed that of God.

Blasphemy!

He whose "understanding is unsearchable" (v. 28) can learn nothing. The vast treasure of his infinite knowledge is beyond any human. "For as the heavens are higher than the earth, so are my ways higher than your ways and my thoughts than your thoughts" (55:9).

Perspective.

Take a step or two back from Isaiah's fortieth chapter for a moment. You'll see that his questions are taken up by the apostle Paul in Romans 11. Consider where the apostle placed them. Having just exhausted all of his Spirit-given wisdom and revelation in describing the wonder of God's grace to mankind (Rom. 1–11), the apostle threw up his hands and, nearly beside himself, declared himself unable to put human words around the greatness and grace of God. Hear how he falls back upon Isaiah's questions:

> Oh, the depth of the riches and wisdom and knowledge of God! How unsearchable are his judgments and how inscrutable his ways!
> "For who has known the mind of the Lord,
>   or who has been his counselor?"
> "Or who has given a gift to him
>   that he might be repaid?"

> For from him and through him and to him are all things.
> To him be glory forever. Amen.

(Rom. 11:33–36)

Perspective. Life is all about perspective. When we see rightly, we worship reverently. When we don't, we descend into worry, pity, and bitterness. Take your pick. You can live your life either way.

## Reflect on these points

1. *Fresh perspective does not change the facts. It only brings them within our view.*

2. *A well-timed, well-stated question is often God's way of changing our perspective. What question is God placing on your heart right now?*

3. *Sometimes what we need most is not the answer we seek, but the questions we avoid. What questions are you failing to ask and what "answer" stands in the way of asking them?*

4. *You are allowed to choose what overwhelms and awes you.*

# The preeminence
of God over
all the nations

*Behold, the nations are like a drop from a bucket, and are accounted as the dust on the scales; behold, he takes up the coastlands like fine dust.*

*Lebanon would not suffice for fuel, nor are its beasts enough for a burnt offering.*

*All the nations are as nothing before him, they are accounted by him as less than nothing and emptiness.*

*Isaiah 40:15–17*

There it is again—that disturbing, arresting, incessant demand: "Behold!" It almost annoys us into realizing that something essential is escaping our attention; something that, if missing, will render us less than fully engaged with reality. So urgent is the need and so deep our preoccupation with other matters that Isaiah repeats his demand again before he dares draw another breath.

What is it that we are miscalculating? It is God's preeminent place over all the nations of the earth: "Behold, the nations are like a drop from a bucket."

At the time of writing there are 192 sovereign nations of the world. From Laos to Luxembourg. From Venezuela to Vanuatu. From the United States of America to the United Arab Emirates. All of them are full of their own versions of pomp, pride, and patriotism.

By "the nations" Isaiah likely meant, not so much political entities, but peoples and kingdoms as defined in his day. The flags and borders may have changed, but the point is the same.

God resides over, above, and in control of them all. Today the nations number nearly 200. Presumably in Isaiah's mind he saw far fewer. But God knew the nations of the world then and he knows them now. They are individually and collectively "like a drop from a bucket" before him. That is to say, they are insignificant, not in the sense that God is callous toward them, but that he is not moved by their glory. It is not that he doesn't care, but that he has no regard for their supposed might, autonomy, and power. Isaiah's statement is not a sign of God's indifference toward them, but of their non-intimidation toward him.

No one notices a drop from a bucket. The water sloshes and sways and a drop is flung from the bucket. Before it can find its way to the ground below, its place has been swallowed up by the surrounding molecules and is remembered no more. A nanosecond later the drop splats into the dust and within moments is absorbed so thoroughly as to be invisible to any who might try to find its whereabouts. The lifespan of a drop of water is in direct proportion to the rate of its descent and the distance from its demise.

So are the nations of the world before God. It is true that, when God acts out of his grace, we read, "God so loved the world, that he gave his only Son" (John 3:16). But it is also true that, when the nations act out of some self-perceived autonomy, "the nations are like a drop from a bucket."

Isaiah probably had in view the armed forces of the nations that surrounded Judah. Remember the awesome display of military might they had just witnessed Assyria unleash upon their brothers to the north. Remember the massive foreign military power which encircled Jerusalem (Isa. 36–37). Remember its great downfall (37:36–38)? The most powerful nation on the face of the earth had been decimated by God silently, under the cover of night. Surely the prophet also had Babylon in view—the nation which would fill the void left in the international bucket of nations by the removal of Assyria. It would one day be the conqueror of Judah and become her place of exile. It would also be the land (though later herself conquered by the Persians) from which they would return to a brighter future (48:20).

Now, in view of what God had just done to Assyria, and in view of what his people would yet face at the hand of the nation of nations, Isaiah demands that they fix reality firmly in their view.

Remember the strategy of the US military as they invaded Iraq? "Shock and awe." It was all the news media could talk about for weeks leading up to the invasion. Shock and awe: a demonstration of military might so overwhelming, so overpowering, so devastating that it demoralizes and paralyzes the opposing troops. Indeed, the display that followed was awesome.

We do well to remember, however, that even at its greatest, no human army—be it from the USA, Assyria, Babylon, or any other nation—shocks or awes God. Indeed, such armies, to change the metaphor, "are accounted as the dust on the scales." They are weightless, inconsequential, irrelevant. Any merchant on the streets of Jerusalem, before making a sale, would have taken his standardized weights from the balance. The fine dust that blew in with the breeze was not worthy of concern. But if a customer quibbled, the merchant might send a puff of breath across the surface of the scale and the dust was gone.

Thus are the nations in the estimation of our God! "[B]ehold, he takes up the coastlands like fine dust."

Think of the nations in their greatest glory: the USSR and the USA at the height of the cold war, Hitler and his Third Reich during their most daunting advance, Babylon, Greece, Rome of old. They were—and others still are—as nothing before God. They do not derail him from his purposes. They are powerless and inconsequential to the ultimate outcome of human history. History is indeed "his story"!

Stockpile all the natural resources bequeathed by God to the nations and they are not sufficient to draw his attention. "Lebanon would not suffice for fuel, nor are its beasts enough for a burnt offering." If every tree in Lebanon's vast, rich forests were to be cut and burned in a sacrificial fire to God, it would not impress him. If every beast in those forests were burned upon that fire, it would not move God.

"All the nations are as nothing before him, they are accounted by him as less than nothing and emptiness." The expression "less than nothing" translates a Hebrew word meaning "to cease," "to fail," and "to come to an end." The word "emptiness" describes formlessness and confusion. When the nations are made to stand before God, their purposes fail and their plans crumble.

"Impressive," you might say, "but so what? I'm not worried about international diplomacy!"

Fair question. You may not be worried about the nations of the world, but something *does* appear to threaten you. It makes tomorrow look uncertain and the will of God unattainable. It shocks your system and awes your mind. It overwhelms your thinking, emasculates your will, and saps your strength. I can't name it specifically, but you know it by name. In fact, I'm guessing you're picturing it at this precise moment.

Know this: God owns it. Whatever it is, God controls it. He is sovereign over it. Your Father makes that which overwhelms you to serve *his* purposes. You may not understand it, but he does. You may not be able to control it, but he does. You may think you can't survive it, but he has promised you on this side of the terror that he *can* bring you through ... and *will*, if you will but get the eyes of your heart full of him.

The great nation of Babylon would threaten Judah. It would become the nightmare to the nations that Assyria only dreamed of being. And God would use these ruthless pagan armies to discipline his people by taking them into exile. It was unthinkable to a Jewish mind. Yet God wanted his people to know from the beginning of those terrors that he was in complete control of them. The nation that would appear so all-powerful was in fact under his sovereign direction from start to finish. He wanted them to never lose sight of the fact that he was making the wrath of man to praise him and serve his purposes (Ps. 76:10).

God would allow Babylon to ascend to the zenith of *her* glory so he could use her greatest king to demonstrate the greatness of *his* glory. The name Nebuchadnezzar looms so large over the history of Babylon that no other single word more aptly summarizes its glory and power. Yet a century after Isaiah's day, when Nebuchadnezzar took to himself a greatness reserved for God alone (Dan. 4:30), God laid this king of Babylon low. After seven years, God restored Nebuchadnezzar's sanity and he confessed:

> At the end of the days I, Nebuchadnezzar, lifted my
> eyes to heaven, and my reason returned to me, and I
> blessed the Most High, and praised and honored
> him who lives forever,
> for his dominion is an everlasting dominion,
>   and his kingdom endures from generation to
>     generation;
> all the inhabitants of the earth are accounted
>     as nothing [sounds like Isaiah, doesn't it?],
>   and he does according to his will among the host
>     of heaven
>   and among the inhabitants of the earth;
> and none can stay his hand
>   or say to him, "What have you done?"
>
> (Dan. 4:34–35)

Whatever it is that threatens hope—*your* hope—God knows it and owns it. Whatever makes tomorrow uncertain, God has already written the last line.

So rest. Get your eyes and heart full of him. Let your heart be at peace.

## Reflect on these points

1. *Chances are that whatever seems all-powerful at present is in fact inconsequential to the fulfillment of God's purposes. Take some time to tell God of your worst fears. Conclude by expressing thanks for his all-encompassing sovereignty.*

2. *Whatever shocks and awes your heart is unimpressive to God. Turn to a season of worship, extolling God in his greatness and allowing all that seems so overwhelming in this life to find its measure before his throne.*

3. *Whatever overwhelms you, know that God owns it, controls it, and is sovereign over it.*

# The preeminence
# of God over
# all the idols

*To whom then will you liken God, or what likeness compare with him?*

*An idol! A craftsman casts it, and a goldsmith overlays it with gold and casts for it silver chains.*

*He who is too impoverished for an offering chooses wood that will not rot; he seeks out a skillful craftsman to set up an idol that will not move.*

*Isaiah 40:18–20*

The demand to "Behold your God" is at once both arresting and superfluous. It stops us short because none of us naturally fix our eyes upon God in his glory. Yet we all have a deity in our gaze. Isaiah's call is not to turn from secular sight to spiritual sight, but to divert our adoring fascination from a false god to the true God.

This is precisely why he puts to us another question: "To whom then will you liken God, or what likeness compare with him?" Isaiah's question here will become the question directly from God's own mouth: "To whom then will you compare me, that I should be like him? says the Holy One" (v. 25).

We are all worshipers. We are no more able to rid ourselves of the worship reflex than we can decide not to breath. It is in our DNA to worship. We are not free to not worship. Ours is merely the decision of what or whom we will worship. Isaiah's question is not, "Are you likening something to God?" He is unmasking any current idolatry: "To whom then will you compare me, that I should be like him?"

Isaiah's frightened countrymen stood with mouths agape, speechless before the question. So the prophet answered for them: "An idol!"

The shame of having "exchanged the glory of the immortal God for images resembling mortal man and birds and animals and reptiles" (Rom. 1:23) was more than they could explain away. So Isaiah continued, "A craftsman casts it, and a goldsmith overlays it with gold and casts for it silver chains. He who is too impoverished for an offering chooses wood that will not rot; he seeks out a skillful craftsman to set up an idol that will not move."

Rich or poor—we all find something to worship. Gold or silver, oak or pine—it matters not; our impulse to worship will not be stopped. Each one "chooses" his or her idol. The verb is a curious one. It is used throughout the Hebrew Scriptures to describe divine choice—God's election of Abraham, Israel, the Levites, Aaron, David, and others.[1] God's will rules. His choice trumps all others. Here, however, the worshiper is seen as sovereign over his god—electing his idol of choice to an altar of worship.

Idols, of course, come in all shapes and sizes ... and even without any shape or size whatsoever. Idols may be sexual (1 Cor. 6:9) or monetary (Eph. 5:5; Col. 3:5) in nature. We may bow down before the altar of our appetites (Phil. 3:19) or of our pleasures (2 Tim. 3:4). Our ingenuity in idolatry is nearly infinite.

The most hideous of idols are not those crafted in the shape of an animal or astral gods (as per the Babylonians), but those which are distortions of the true and living God, passed off in his name. The very gift that God extends to us in his grace can become the object of our worship. The service of God can become an idol-god. Our distortion of God, perhaps attractive because of cultural shifts or personal peccadilloes, is nevertheless not God. A caricature of God is not God, but a false god wearing a cheap mask of the divine. Tozer was correct:

> Let us beware lest we in our pride accept the erroneous notion that idolatry consists only in kneeling before visible objects of adoration, and that civilized peoples are therefore free from it. The essence of idolatry is the entertainment of thoughts about God that are unworthy of him. It begins in the mind and may be present where no overt act of worship has taken place ... Wrong ideas about God are not only the fountain from which the polluted waters of idolatry flow; they are themselves idolatrous. The idolater simply imagines things about God and acts as if they were true.[2]

Suddenly Isaiah is speaking to us. What gods have you fashioned to sit atop the altars of convenience and comfort? What garish, brilliantly lit god have you set before you? With what neon-flash have you adorned God's neck and diminished him into a god of your own making? How have you pulled God down to your understanding? A god who is understood entirely is not worthy of our worship.

My closest brush with what we might call classic idolatry came while standing next to a mud hole in West Africa. My wife and I were deep in the heart of the city of Bobo-Dioulasso in Burkina Faso. Our guides were two single missionary nurses. Having pulled over and exited the car we suddenly found ourselves surrounded by a swelling throng of half-clad children. They were shouting, one voice atop another, some indecipherable request. I looked helplessly at our guides. It took them a moment to make sense of the cacophony of voices, but soon one turned toward me with a strange expression and said, "They want to know if we want to see the sacred fish." I quizzically looked at her with an expression which said, "I don't know, do we?" Then, before I really knew what I was saying, I replied, "Sure, why not!"

A shout of glee went up when she translated my desire. The throng engulfed us and moved us down a street and in between buildings, through twisting narrows between ramshackle mud huts in a labyrinth of dizzying directions. I started to fear we were being taken to a trap or that, if abandoned by the crowd, we would never be able to find our way back. But soon the claustrophobic back alleys gave way to a more open, barren ditch, surrounded by houses. The merry multitude escorted us to the bottom of the ditch. There we came upon a trickle of water not more than three feet wide at any one point. It was the color of chocolate milk and appeared to be about the consistency of motor oil—a stewed concoction of water, dead grass, and sewage. I noted a naked girl squatting in the muddy waters just downstream, clearly in the middle of her bath. This, I would soon discover, served as dishwater, urinal, bathtub, and water supply for the people of the area.

The crowd came to a halt and the jabber increased in both volume and reverence. Looking up at one of our missionary friends I heard her say, "This is where the sacred fish is supposed to be." I peered down at a place where the water had pooled into a round area hardly wide enough to require a gentle leap to cross. As I took in the scene I thought to myself, "Nothing could live in that mess!"

A silent, rapt wonder came over the children as they gazed intently at the still surface of the water. We were instructed to stand silently and wait—the sacred fish would appear in due time. We waited among the adoring horde. Then suddenly I saw the slightest ripple move across the surface of the water and heard an ecstatic cry rise up from the children. "The sacred fish! The sacred fish!" they squealed with rapturous delight as they jumped up and down.

However, a sad sense of wonder passed over me. I'd read of such idolatry. I'd pictured it as I read the sacred pages of Scripture. But here I beheld it firsthand for the first time. I was not certain just how to process my feelings. These dear people, created by and precious to God, were worshiping the creature rather than the Creator. He had fashioned each of them with the capacity for such affections, but here they were offering them at an unworthy altar to an unworthy god. How God's heart must have been breaking!

In time, however, I began to reflect upon the more refined idols of my own heart. I began to see the gods that have vied for the worship offered on the altars of my mind, heart, calendar, and bank accounts. Unlike ever before, I saw the detestable nature of *my* idolatrous heart. I began to see that the shiny gods to whom I bring the offerings of my time, attention, longing, labors, and sacrifice are no more worthy of my sacrifices, attention, and worship than that unfortunate fish. My heart began to bring into focus, not just the darkness of these children's idolatry, but also the disgusting nature of my own misplaced affections and adoration.

Idolatry is something even Christian hearts must flee (1 Cor. 10:14). Fleeing idolatry is not a flight from worship, but from worship wrongly directed. It is not a refusal to bow down, to do homage and obeisance to another, but is the choice to give such heart-devotion only to the true God. Fleeing idolatry is not simply running away from something, it is running to someone—God in his glory. In our continuing flight, idolatry is something we must constantly guard our hearts against (1 John 5:21). We guard our hearts from idolatry not by building a wall and shutting everything out. We guard our hearts most perfectly when we sign them over to the God of gods—and make our hearts his inner sanctuary.

It may just be that tomorrow looks uncertain because you have laid it at the altar of an unworthy god. Take it up; bring it to "the everlasting God" (Isa. 40:28) and see if it does not look different when he owns it. Pray with William Cowper,

The dearest idol I have known,
Whate'er that idol be,
Help me to tear it from thy throne,
And worship only thee.[3]

## Reflect on these points

1. *We are not free to be worship-free. Ours is merely the decision of what or whom we will worship. In the midst of your current worries and fears, where is the attention of your heart directed?*

2. *Our distortion of God is not God, but an idol passed off in his name. If you were to view a log of your actual thoughts of God over the past week, what doctrine would it represent?*

3. *Fleeing idolatry is not a flight from worship, but from worship wrongly directed. Have you in some way drawn a caricature of God in your heart?*

4. *The reason why tomorrow looks uncertain may be because you have laid it at the altar of an unworthy god. Ask God to illuminate your heart to see with fresh eyes the truth of who he is.*

# The preeminence
## of God over
## all the rulers

*Do you not know? Do you not hear? Has it not been told you from the beginning? Have you not understood from the foundations of the earth?*

*It is he who sits above the circle of the earth, and its inhabitants are like grasshoppers; who stretches out the heavens like a curtain, and spreads them like a tent to dwell in;*

*who brings princes to nothing, and makes the rulers of the earth as emptiness.*

*Scarcely are they planted, scarcely sown, scarcely has their stem taken root in the earth, when he blows on them, and they wither, and the tempest carries them off like stubble.*

**Isaiah 40:21–24**

God is preeminent over all things—the earth, the nations, the idols. But our problems are often far more personal than that. They have faces, names, and frequent enough contact with you to make your life miserable. Some call them power-people. They have control, authority, power, leverage, influence, clout, and connections. They command, direct, dictate, dominate, and issue decrees. They are encountered in nearly every sphere of life: work, school, community, athletics, politics—even church and home. The whole of our lives at times appears to reside within the sweep of their whims and wishes.

For Isaiah and his countrymen the name that had instilled more fear than any other was Sennacherib, king of Assyria. God, however, had proven his supremacy over this most powerful man on earth (Isa. 37:36–38). But soon enough there was a new face, a new name, and a new nation threatening. Hezekiah once again doubted God's ability to deal with the power of the king of Babylon (ch. 39). Despite God's faithfulness in the past, the present person of power can still incite fear and trembling.

Isaiah was not writing just for his own day, but also for his people when they were in exile, under the power of the king of Babylon. Then they would need to know the preeminence of God over ever power-person, particularly the king of Babylon, who would appear nearly omnipotent to them. We, no less than they, need such a perspective.

Isaiah calls four questions into his service. He does so because a question mark can often pull off what a period cannot. Where a statement stalls, a question frequently plows a trail. The waters are starting to run deep, so Isaiah pulls out these questions to keep us from losing the trail God has put us on: "Do you not know? Do you not hear? Has it not been told you from the beginning? Have you not understood from the foundations of the earth?"

These are, of course, rhetorical questions—that is to say, they do not expect an audible answer. They are designed to make us think, not answer. Their purpose is to grow our understanding, not confirm our suspicions. They are put to us so that we will realize we have been missing something— something we should have understood long ago. "There was a time," said Reinhold Niebuhr, "when I had all the answers.

My real growth began when I discovered that the questions to which I had the answers were not the important questions."[1]

There is something even more dangerous than not possessing answers to our questions. It is being cocksure of our answers to questions that ultimately do not matter. So Isaiah seeks first to deliver us from our answers so we can learn to ask the right questions. The right questions are about the preeminence of God—in this case, questions about his supremacy over all the power-people of the earth. That is where Isaiah is taking us, but he begins first by grabbing us by the scruff of the neck and yanking us upward: "It is he who sits above the circle of the earth, and its inhabitants are like grasshoppers; who stretches out the heavens like a curtain, and spreads them like a tent to dwell in."

By "the circle of the earth," Isaiah refers to the semi-circular appearance of the curvature of the earth at the place where heaven and earth meet. God sits above the juncture of heaven and earth and is Lord over both. From this vantage point the earth's "inhabitants are like grasshoppers." As grasshoppers appear to us, so all humans (including the power-people) appear to God. The words "inhabitants," "sits," and "dwell in" are all translations of the same Hebrew word. God "sits above the circle of the earth" looking down upon those who sit in exalted fashion over their grasshopper-kingdom.

So?

He who is so enthroned is the One "who brings princes to nothing, and makes the rulers of the earth as emptiness."

God has absolute sway over the mightiest of earth's people. There are no power-people in God's eyes. The word translated "princes" means to be weighty, judicious, or commanding.[2] The word translated "rulers" describes a law-giver, judge or governor.[3] The realm of their weight and power is "of the earth." They may manipulate and coerce on this plain, but they do not touch God or his throne. As the nations are "as nothing before him" (v. 17), so are their rulers. The nations are "emptiness" before him (v. 17), and so are their power-people.

Such people are like transitory seed in the hands of the Lord of the harvest. Their entire life-cycle is in his hand. By his will "are they planted" and "sown." He makes "their stem [take] root in the earth" and he causes them to "wither." He sees to it that "the tempest carries them off like stubble." His hand plants them in this life. His will allows them to take root and grow, determining the place of their habitation, the breadth of their foliage, and the abundance of their fruit. Soon enough, "he blows on them, and they wither." The breath of the Lord was pictured earlier as bringing all flesh to an end (v. 7). Their advantages do them no good before the word of judgment that proceeds from God's mouth. One day Christ will return and the people of power will behold that "From his mouth comes a sharp sword with which to strike down the nations, and he will rule them with a rod of iron. He will tread the winepress of the fury of the wrath of God the Almighty" (Rev. 19:15).

Like a sirocco sweeping over arid desert sands, this judgment consumes them. Before the breath of God's mouth they "wither" and "the tempest carries them off like stubble." They who once appeared all-powerful will have the juices of life sapped from their bodies, be reduced to dust, and will be gone with the wind.

Can God really do this? Will he?

After Sennacherib's envoy boasted that not even the Lord could deliver Jerusalem (Isa. 36:18–20), God wiped out 185,000 of his troops in one silent night of disaster (37:36) and sent the king home to face his own demise (v. 38).

Could God do this with the king of Babylon, the new intimidator? That king would one day say of himself, "I am, and there is no one besides me" (47:8, 10). This was God's self-declaration of sovereignty, used over twenty times in Isaiah 41–46.[4] Over him God decreed a great downfall:

> These two things shall come to you
>   in a moment, in one day;
> the loss of children and widowhood
>   shall come upon you in full measure,
> in spite of your many sorceries
>   and the great power of your enchantments ...
> But evil shall come upon you,
>   which you will not know how to charm away;
> disaster shall fall upon you,
>   for which you will not be able to atone;
> and ruin shall come upon you suddenly,
>   of which you know nothing.
>
>                                        (47:9, 11)

History records the devastating defeat of the Babylonians before the new world power, Persia. God's Word was kept and the king of Babylon was swept away before a king named Cyrus. To his exiled people, residing under the iron fist of Babylon, God called this king by name long before his birth, so his people would rest assured that his sovereignty extended over the person of power who threatened them. God said "of Cyrus, 'He is my shepherd, and he shall fulfill all my purpose'; saying of Jerusalem, 'She shall be built,' and of the temple, 'Your foundation shall be laid'" (Isa. 44:28). God called Cyrus his "anointed" (45:1)—the same designation given to Saul and David (1 Sam. 10:1; 2 Sam. 23:1)—and his "chosen ally" (48:14–15, NIV).

How could God call a pagan king his "shepherd," "anointed," and "chosen ally"? Because God owned him. Behold, "The king's heart is a stream of water in the hand of the LORD; he turns it wherever he will" (Prov. 21:1)!

God used the Assyrians to discipline the people of the northern kingdom of Israel. Once they had done so, God removed them at the hands of the Babylonians, whom he used to discipline the southern kingdom of Judah. He removed the Babylonians by raising up the Persians, whose king he used to bring back his people from exile to their land of promise with a commission to rebuild the temple in Jerusalem (2 Chr. 36:22–23; Ezra 1:1–4). *And God predicted all of this beforehand* so that his people would never lose sight of his preeminence over all earthly power-people.

Stalin, Mao Tse-Tung, Hitler, Idi Amin, Pol Pot—the mere

mention of their names sends a chill down one's spine. But they are gone; dust in the wind. No one in your realm of experience will be any different. God rules all, and all will answer to him.

A day is coming when a loud voice from heaven will declare once and for all, "The kingdom of the world has become the kingdom of our Lord and of his Christ, and he shall reign forever and ever" (Rev. 11:15). For now, *that* face, *that* name, *that* person remains. But know this: God rules even that person, even now. Know that God knows your plight. And until that time, rest in the knowledge that there are no power-people from where God sits.

## Reflect on these points

*1. As grasshoppers appear to us, so the power-people in your life appear to God. Have you been living more consistently in the fear of God or the fear of man?*

*2. God owns the one who appears most threatening to you, to your plans, to your well-being, and to your loved ones. Entrust them once again to him in a season of prayer.*

*3. It is as easy for God to accomplish his will through rebellious people of seemingly unlimited power as it is for him to accomplish it through your willing, submissive service.*

# The preeminence
## of God over
### all the heavens

*To whom then will you compare me, that I should be like him? says the Holy One.*

*Lift up your eyes on high and see: who created these? He who brings out their host by number, calling them all by name, by the greatness of his might, and because he is strong in power not one is missing.*

*Isaiah 40:25–26*

What a difference a few degrees can make! Change the angle of your head just slightly and your entire world changes. Lift your eyes a mere forty-five degrees and take in what has been there all along. You're willing to throw your head back to swallow a few tranquilizers. Do it again—this time without the pills—and linger long enough to look up.

The question earlier posed by Isaiah (40:18) now confronts us straight from the mouth of God himself: "To whom then will you compare me, that I should be like him?" In case you are tempted to slough off the question too casually, remember it is "the Holy One" who puts it to you.[1] Refusing to answer is not an option.

What, no answer? In the awkward silence, Isaiah offers a suggestion: "Lift up your eyes on high and see." And what is it you do see? Scientists estimate that the visible universe is a million million million million miles across. Maybe the Arabic numerals will help: that's 1,000,000,000,000,000,000,000,000,000 miles![2] Remember, light travels at approximately 186,000 miles *per second*. Recalibrate your thinking. Oh, and by the way, you might want to fasten your seat belt as well. If you launched off from Planet Earth at that speed you would pass the moon around a minute later, about the time you hopefully would be catching your breath. Keep up the pace and you'd pass the sun in just over eight minutes. If you are up to it, another mere 80,000 years at 186,000 miles per second will get you to the far side of our little galaxy. And all of that is within your view with just a tilt of the head.

With your naked eye you can only see around 6,000 stars, and only 2,000 of those are within your view from any one place you might choose to stand. Rummage through the closet and pull out the binoculars and you'll be able to bring about 50,000 stars into view.[3] But you're only getting started. Scientists estimate the total number of stars in just our galaxy is between 100 billion and 400 billion. But remember, there are approximately 140 billion other such galaxies out there, each one with an estimated one billion stars within it.[4] The total number of stars may actually be somewhere between $10^{22}$ and $10^{24}$.[5]

Starting to get the picture? Since God's question stumped us, listen to the one Isaiah follows up with after having raised the level of our sight: "[W]ho created these?"

*Gulp.*

Keep your eyes upward and let me keep going. Let's try to build a scale model of just our little solar system. Pick a single pea from your dinner plate—make that Planet Earth. According to scale, Jupiter would be over a thousand feet away, and you'd have to walk a mile and a half before you could set down Pluto (don't worry, it wouldn't be too heavy—about the size of a bacterium). At this same scale our closest neighbor-star would be about ten thousand miles from our little pea-sized earth. That's just our solar system. Realize that the average distance between stars is estimated to be twenty million million miles.[6]

Before we get lost in space and forget our question, let me ask again: Who created these?

*More silence?*

Then let Isaiah answer: "He who brings out their host by number, calling them all by name, by the greatness of his might, and because he is strong in power not one is missing."

Mark his words carefully. He refers to the heavenly bodies arrayed before you as a "host." This was a military term used to describe the vast, innumerable armies of a nation. It is surely just what the Assyrian armies appeared to be when they encircled Jerusalem (Isa. 36–37). But Hezekiah had turned the word toward heaven and called God the "LORD of hosts" (37:16) and confessed to him, "you have made heaven and earth."

Head back, eyes open, mind engaged—God made everything you see, and all that is beyond your vision. He spoke them into being, he set them in space, he dispatched them in their orbits, and he governs their regularity. Stars and planets, time and space, the vast unsearchable reaches of the great unknown—they all snap to attention at his command. "[H]e upholds the universe by the word of his power" (Heb. 1:3) and "in him all things hold together" (Col. 1:17).

The Babylonians of old were renowned for their worship of the stars and the astral gods they assigned to them. They took both astronomy and astrology to new levels. If they had obeyed Isaiah's command to "Lift up your eyes on high and see," their pagan eyes would have seen a multiplicity of gods who were identified with the countless stars in space, gods who controlled the earth and its inhabitants and whose wills and whims could be known by studying those stars. It was to Babylon that Isaiah's people would one day go in exile. God wanted his people to know before they ever arrived that he rules not only the stars with which their captors were fascinated, but also the gods they had assigned to them. Their destiny did not reside in the course of the stars, the stages of the planets or the predictions of the horoscope. Their destiny was still, despite their circumstances, firmly in the grip of God's hand. The Babylonians lifted their eyes and saw gods. The people of God are to lift their eyes and see God's glory arrayed before them (Ps. 19:1–6).

If you could convince your contemporaries to obey Isaiah's command and "Lift up [their] eyes on high and see," they would tell you that they behold the glories of the god of naturalism. "You need not postulate the presence of a Creator," they would tell you. In worshipful tones of rapt wonder they would comfort you, "It just happened."

In your present pilgrimage upon this fallen earth (Heb.

11:13; 1 Peter 1:1, 17), God wishes to remind you that, despite popular opinion and current scientific hypotheses, he created, owns, and governs the heavens and the earth. He is still "the LORD of hosts." He is still the Maker of heaven and earth upon whom Hezekiah called and who miraculously brought him deliverance (Isa. 37:16).

The world was shocked on Saturday, February 1, 2003 to hear the sad news of the disastrous explosion of Space Shuttle *Columbia* as it made its descent to earth. All seven occupants perished. Later that day President George W. Bush addressed the nation with words of perspective and hope:

> In the skies today, we saw destruction and tragedy. Yet farther than we can see, there is comfort and hope. In the words of the prophet Isaiah, "Lift up your eyes and look to the heavens. Who created all these? He who brings out the starry hosts one by one and calls them each by name. Because of his great power and mighty strength, not one of them is missing." The same creator who names the stars also knows the names of the seven souls we mourn today. The crew of the shuttle Columbia did not return safely to Earth, yet we can pray that all are safely home.[7]

Each morning the crew of the *Columbia* was awakened by music piped in from Mission Control in Houston. The families of the various crew members took turns selecting the music for the morning's wakeup call. On January 21, just days before the tragedy, *Columbia* Commander Colonel Rick Husband's family chose the morning's wakeup music. The space shuttle crew awakened to an exalted vista of the earth afforded only a few mortals and to the sounds of these words:

> Lord of all creation
> Of water, earth and sky
> The heavens are your tabernacle
> Glory to the Lord on high.
> God of wonders beyond our galaxy
> You are holy, holy
> The universe displays your majesty
> You are holy, holy
> Lord of heaven and earth.[8]

Your days of physical life may be few. Tomorrow may not come. If it doesn't—and even if it does—is your life in the hand of the Lord of heaven and earth?

### Reflect on these points

1. *Might we say that in some sense God created the heavens in order to help us take right measure of our conditions upon the earth? Look up and ponder your troubles with new perspective.*

2. *A few moments of God-empowered, heaven-directed reflection can displace earth-bound anxieties. Make some time for extended reflection on Isaiah 40:25–26.*

3. *The God who created the vastness of outer space can rule the complexities of your inner space. If possible,*

*spend some time under a clear night sky. Praise God for his sovereignty over both it and you.*

4. *Take a moment to express your worship to God, and then in fresh surrender submit to him your concerns about tomorrow.*

# The presence of God

*Get you up to a high mountain, O Zion, herald of good news; lift up your voice with strength, O Jerusalem, herald of good news; lift it up, fear not; say to the cities of Judah, "Behold your God!"*

*Isaiah 40:9*

When once God's preeminence is established in your eyes, his presence can be manifest in your heart. In theological jargon this means that God's transcendence and his immanence cannot be separated. The joyful experience of the latter follows infallibly upon the glad recognition of the former.

God is everywhere. God is here—wherever *here* is for you at this precise moment. There is no place where God is not. He is present in the fullness of his Being at every point in his creation. Theologians call this God's "omnipresence." We all always exist in the presence of God. As the apostle Paul told the idolaters of Athens, "In him we live and move and have our being" (Acts 17:28). But as Tozer reminds us,

> The Presence and the manifestation of the Presence are not the same. There can be the one without the other. God is here when we are wholly unaware of it. He is manifest only when and as we are aware of His presence … If we cooperate with Him in loving obedience, God will manifest Himself to us, and that manifestation will be the difference between a nominal Christian life and a life radiant with the light of His face.[1]

How can we move from the *knowledge* that God is present to the *experience* of his presence? What will make the difference between simply dotting our theological "i"s and crossing our doctrinal "t"s and actually encountering the manifest presence of God?

We cooperate with God when we recognize the spiritual pattern he has established for relationship with his people. Note the word *relationship*—this is not merely about maxims and propositions concerning God. This is warm, interactive, loving relationship. This is beyond simply knowing *about* God. This is knowing *God*. In English, when we speak of "knowing," it often describes little more than information reserves accumulated about this or that person, place, or thing. The Hebrew concept of knowledge, however, is warm, experiential, and charged with life. The Hebrew word designates, not a cold linkage of cognitions and postulations, but a vital, intimate relationship of communion. The spiritual pattern for moving into this kind of relationship with God is seen throughout the Scriptures.

David spoke of it in Psalm 22. He felt as if God was distant: "My God, my God, why have you forsaken me? Why are you so far from saving me, from the words of my groaning? O my God, I cry by day, but you do not answer, and by night, but I find no rest" (vv. 1–2). No other psalm more powerfully depicts the sufferings of Jesus on the cross. Though the words find their ultimate fulfillment in Christ, you feel—albeit with lesser intensity and for a different purpose—as if you've been there.

You have repeatedly affirmed him as "My God," and you have done so "by day" and "by night," but still he seems distant. You want out of this cycle, just as David did. King David's next words reveal that he knew the path up and out of that pit: "Yet you are holy, enthroned on the praises of Israel" (v. 3).

The picture is of the Lord's manifest presence made known in the tabernacle or temple. His presence was said to dwell above the mercy seat between the wings of the cherubim in the holy of holies. But here the more usual "cherubim" is replaced with "the praises" of his people. The word translated "enthroned" means simply to sit, remain, or dwell.[2] The implication is clear: God makes himself at home where he is rightly exalted and worshiped. As H. C. Leupold wrote, "[T]he praises of the faithful … are the new throne above which He resides."[3]

When God's preeminence is established in your heart, his presence is manifest in your life. Those throughout the ages who have discovered the manifest presence of God have repeatedly testified to the constancy of this pattern. "The LORD is *near* to all who call on him, to all who call on him *in truth*" (Ps. 145:18, emphasis added). This is not about throwing aside solid theology; it is about experiencing the One whom good theology describes. Is this not what James demanded in the New Testament? "Draw near to God, and he will draw near to you" (James 4:8). The fact is, you are as close to God as you want to be. Not because you possess what it takes to enter the presence of God, but because in Christ he has removed every obstacle to your coming. He has thrown the door open and invited you to enter.

God's preeminence in your heart opens the door to the manifestation of his presence in your life. This is precisely the note upon which Isaiah concludes his prophecy:

> Thus says the LORD: "Heaven is my throne,
>> and the earth is my footstool [this is the preeminent
>>> transcendence of God];
> what is the house that you would build for me,
>> and what is the place of my rest?
> All these things my hand has made,
>> and so all these things came to be,
>>> declares the LORD.
> But this is the one to whom I will look:
> he who is humble and contrite in spirit
> and trembles at my word [this is the immanent nearness
>> of God]"
>
> (Isa. 66:1–2)

The preeminence and presence of God converge in the life consumed with the glory of God.

Such folk confess with David, "the nearness of God is my good" (Ps. 73:28, NASB). They testify, "Blessed is the one you choose and bring near, to dwell in your courts!" (65:4a). They cry, "a day in your courts is better than a thousand elsewhere" (84:10a). There is nothing like the presence of God.

Isaiah was concerned that God's exiled people not lose the hope of God's manifest presence. Through the years of exile in a foreign land those Jews began to lose a functional use of their mother-tongue. Thus some began to translate/paraphrase the Scriptures into the more familiar Aramaic, and the result is called the Targums. At that time they began to speak of the manifestation of God's presence as the *shekinah*—an Aramaic word taken from the verb "to dwell," from which in turn came the word for "tabernacle." The God who had manifested himself on behalf of his people in the past would again dwell with his people.

It was a seismic shift, therefore, when John said of Jesus, "the Word became flesh and dwelt [lit. "tabernacled"] among us, and we have seen his glory ..." (John 1:14). God had again manifested himself—this time not in a cloud by day and a pillar of fire by night, but in a human body. God was manifest in Christ! And to those who by faith would embrace this Christ as God manifest—as their Redeemer, Savior, and Lord—he promised, "Whoever has my commandments and keeps them, he it is who loves me. And he who loves me will be loved by my Father, and I will love him and *manifest myself to him*" (John 14:21, emphasis added). The manifestation that began with Christ in human flesh is now perpetuated through the continuing work of the Holy Spirit as he mediates the life of the ascended Christ to us who are his body (see John 16:13–15). He seeks to manifest himself in us until together we are "filled with all the fullness of God" (Eph. 3:19). Indeed, he who manifested God's presence in the temple of his physical body (John

2:21) has now made us his temple and our hearts his holy of holies (1 Cor. 3:16; 6:19; 2 Cor. 6:16; Eph. 2:21).

This continuing spiritual manifestation of his presence, Jesus said, is conditioned on something from our side. What is this key to the continued manifestation of God's presence in his people? Simply put, it is the exaltation of Christ to the preeminent place in our lives through our absolute obedience to his Word. Some are quick to equate God's manifest presence with a certain style of worship, a certain kind of doctrine, or a certain type of religious agenda. God manifesting his presence where his preeminence is established does not bind him to an assured form of manifestation. If God is truly preeminent in our lives, he is so, not because he resides in our preconceived boxes, but because he has secured our obedience. In exalting God's preeminence we must realize that his manifest presence may well not validate our agendas, but threaten them—seeking to replace them with far more holy and healthy agendas. When God's preeminence is established in our lives through explicit obedience, his presence is known in our hearts. And it is known in whatever way he in his preeminence deems appropriate.

On the other hand, when God's presence is not known in some clear way among us who call ourselves by his Name, it likely means that we have magnified lesser gods. We have filled our mind's eye with puny gods of our own imagination. We have found our delight in gods of our own making, rather than in the God who made us. We have either given God's place to other gods (be they sensual, monetary, or our appetites) or we have redrawn him into a diminished god of our own rendering. And thus he stands at a distance (relationally) and lets our affair with idolatry run its course. He does not reject us forever, but stands brokenheartedly at a distance. He calls to us, woos us, disciplines us, until such time as we desire him enough to reestablish his preeminence in our lives and dare to draw near.

But this need not be the course you take. God is here. He is near. He will hear as you draw near. He waits in longing, loving jealousy for you to open the door and to allow him the preeminent place in your life: "Behold, I stand at the door and knock. If anyone hears my voice and opens the door, I will come in to him and eat with him, and he with me" (Rev. 3:20).

When once you throw open the door to his preeminence, his presence floods the throne room of your life. This is Isaiah's message of hope. The core of God's preeminence (40:12–26) is wrapped in the manifestation of his presence (vv. 1–11, 27–31). As you prepare your heart for the prospects of his promise, hear Tozer's hopeful words:

> Let us say it again: The universal Presence is a fact. God is here. The whole universe is alive with His life. And He is no strange or foreign God, but the familiar Father of our Lord Jesus Christ whose love has for these thousands of years enfolded the sinful race of men. And always He is trying to get our attention, to reveal Himself to us, to communicate with us. We have within us the ability to know Him if we will but respond to

His overtures. (And this we call pursuing God!) We will know Him in increasing degree as our receptivity becomes more perfect by faith and love and practice.[4]

## Reflect on these points

1. *God's preeminence must be established in your eyes if his presence is to be made known in your heart.*

2. *God makes himself at home where he is rightly and warmly exalted and worshiped. Is this the regular and spontaneous condition of your heart?*

3. *God manifested his presence perfectly in Jesus Christ. You can only know God by surrendering entirely to Jesus. Is this true of you?*

4. *Jesus continues to make his presence known in the temple he is fashioning his people to be. You will never truly know all God has for you without regular, committed involvement with his people. Why has God determined to work this way?*

# The presence of God is our comfort

*Comfort, comfort my people, says your God.*

*Speak tenderly to Jerusalem, and cry to her that her warfare is ended, that her iniquity is pardoned, that she has received from the LORD's hand double for all her sins.*

*Isaiah 40:1–2*

The first word tells the story. The first word after the conflict, the first word after the disagreement, the first word after the discipline has been administered—that first word sets the tone for the rest of the relationship. It casts a hue over the future. That word tells you what tomorrow holds. What was God's first word to Israel for their discipline in exile (Isa. 1–39)? What is God's first word to every repentant, believing heart that runs to God through Jesus?

*Comfort.*

Just to make sure we don't miss it, God doubles it up— "Comfort, comfort my people, says your God." When the preeminent God draws near to manifest his presence you begin to hear his voice, and the first words out of his mouth are "Comfort, comfort ..." Comfort—it's the first word of the rest of your life. Comfort is the label God slaps over your tomorrow.

The origin of the root word behind "comfort" carries the idea of "breathing deeply." Such a breath taken in and released can be a signal of one's emotions.[1] Intriguingly, most of the word's occurrences in the Old Testament speak of what is to us a very different notion. On those occasions the word speaks of

God "repenting" or changing his mind with regard to judgment against sin. This happens, not because God is vacillating, but because he is exceedingly gracious. When a person turns from the sin that must draw God's judgment, God is delighted to turn away his wrath and send forth his loving, covenant grace. To an exiled Israel this would become a breath from heaven whispering the promise of grace to those whose sin had led them into those deserts of their own making. This breath of comforting grace settles over all—of any era, age, race, or nation—who turn back to God from their sin.

It is a command of God Almighty that you hear his word of comfort. God employed an intensive form of the imperative—"Utterly comfort, thoroughly comfort my people!" captures the idea. It is repeated for emphasis. You can hear the ache in God's heart as he draws near to his people. He has not forgotten you. The long silence was not a signal of his lack of interest, but of his loving discipline (Prov. 3:11–12; Heb. 12:5–6).

This was a word for Israel, yet, as the next verses reveal (vv. 3–5), it has a New Testament fulfillment and must be applied to all God's people—Jew and Gentile—who have trusted in Christ. God calls you "my people" and he designates himself "your God." The relationship is not over; it's now on track, restored, revived. You have a future!

The orders are to "Speak tenderly" to Jerusalem. More literally the expression means, "speak to the heart." A direct line from God's heart to yours—no interference, no distractions, nothing to confuse the message. In your heart—

where you think, feel, and choose—at the core of your being, hear God as he comes near! He commands his spokesmen to "cry" his message to you. The declaration is to be bold, vigorous, decisive. There must be no misunderstanding his posture toward you and his message to you! That message is set forth in three metaphors—all of them freeing us from yesterday so we can face tomorrow. Yesterday's sins need not rob today of hope or tomorrow of promise.

### The enmity is over

The picture is a military one: "Cry to her that her warfare is ended." As God comes near, his hands are not rolled into fists. They are open, arms extended to you in an offer of warm embrace.

Our sin has created enmity with God. As Paul would say, we "were by nature children of wrath, like the rest of mankind. But God ..." (Eph. 2:3b–4a). The end of Paul's first sentence parallels Isaiah 1–39: "by nature children of wrath, like the rest of mankind." The beginning of his next sentence wraps up in two words the message of Isaiah 40–66: "But God ..." Our warfare with God is ended! "But God"—no two words could better describe the story of our lives.

The war is over! The enmity is past!

This is no small observation, for Isaiah 40–66 is punctuated twice by a nearly identical refrain: "there is no peace ... for the wicked" (48:22; 57:21). Those two reminders divide Isaiah's twenty-seven chapters of good news into three symmetrical divisions of nine chapters each. These chapters must be understood through eyes illumined by the Holy Spirit, who was given after the cross and resurrection of our Lord. Messianically we meet him here as the all-surpassing God (chs 40–48), the redeeming Servant (chs 49–57), and the reigning King (chs 58–66). Chapters 40–48 reveal God as supreme over all gods.[2] Chapters 49–57 present the culmination of the Servant songs[3] in the greatest prophetic description of the suffering Servant (52:13–53:12). Chapters 58–66 picture God's all-conquering reign, culminating in the new heavens and the new earth (65:17–66:24).

God has ended the enmity created by our sin by establishing his holiness (chs 40–48), atoning for our iniquities (chs 49–57), and ending sin's dominion (chs 58–66). This is God's doing: "LORD, you establish peace for us; all that we have accomplished you have done for us" (26:12, NIV). In the end this peace flows to us like an ever-flowing, never-ending river (66:12). "How beautiful upon the mountains are the feet of him who brings good news, who publishes peace, who brings good news of happiness, who publishes salvation, who says to Zion, 'Your God reigns'" (52:7).

The enmity is over—be at peace!

### The guilt is gone

The picture is a judicial one: "that her iniquity is pardoned" (40:2). God's countenance toward you is not condemnatory. God wears a smile as he looks upon you.

The message to be announced is, more literally, "that her iniquity is accepted." God, in his holiness, can never accept our sin. But he can accept a sacrifice sufficient for our sin. No such sacrifice can arise from human effort: "all our righteous deeds are like a polluted garment" (64:6). But God hints here at what he will make more explicit soon enough—that he himself will provide the sacrifice.

> But he was wounded for our transgressions;
>> he was crushed for our iniquities;
> upon him was the chastisement that brought us peace,
>> and with his stripes we are healed ...
>> the LORD has laid on him
> the iniquity of us all ...
> ... it was the will of the LORD to crush him ...
> ... his soul makes an offering for guilt.
>
> (Isa. 53:5, 6, 10)

These verses looked forward to the atoning work of Christ upon the cross. That offering, having been made and accepted, will never and need never be made again. "Christ also suffered once for sins, the righteous for the unrighteous, that he might bring us to God" (1 Peter 3:18).

The guilt is gone—be at peace!

## The payment is complete

The picture is a commercial one: "that she has received from the LORD's hand double for all her sins" (40:2). God extends more than we deserve. The meaning may be that God has dished out discipline twofold for Israel's sin. But elsewhere the expression looks toward blessings yet to be enjoyed

(61:7). Sin has a wage that is due, and God pays it in full to the unrepentant (Rom. 6:23). But toward his wayward ones mercy always triumphs over judgment (Hab. 3:2).

The picture here is of a lavish grace.[4] A simple correspondence of the sacrifice to the sin would have been sufficient to set our hearts free. And Christ did indeed offer just what was needed for our sins. Yet the perfect sacrifice of the God-man Jesus Christ is not only sufficient, but *abundantly sufficient* for our debt. "In him we have redemption through his blood, the forgiveness of our trespasses, *according to the riches of his grace*" (Eph. 1:7, emphasis added). Note: not "*by* the riches of his grace," but "*according to* the [infinite and immeasurable] riches of his grace"! The grace measured to us in Christ is not simply *out of* a reservoir of divine goodness, but *in proportion to* the limitless measure of the whole of God's infinite grace. Our salvation arises out of "the unsearchable riches of Christ" (Eph. 3:8)!

In the Lord's open, extended hands is "double for all [our] sins." The word "double" can mean to fold over or to fold in half. The same word is used to reveal that God's "true wisdom has two sides" (Job 11:6, NIV)—meaning it exceeds and goes beyond anything humanly comprehensible. There are depths and dimensions to God's wisdom that are not fathomable by human hearts and minds. Thus also God's redeeming grace in Christ deals with the hidden, incalculable dimensions of our sin against a holy God which we could never understand. It releases us into an ocean of grace that is incomprehensible!

Indeed, "where sin increased, grace abounded all the more" (Rom. 5:20)!

The payment is complete—be at peace!

Yesterday's sins and blunders have been decisively dealt with. The long night of divine displeasure has passed and the sun of grace is rising over the horizon of a new day, sending rays of hope and promise over the landscape of tomorrow. Lift your head! Look straight ahead! The enmity is over. The guilt is gone. The punishment is complete. Be comforted … and step forward.

## Reflect on these points

1. *What makes it difficult for you to believe God's first expression to you is a word of comfort?*

2. *In what way do the words "But God …" tell the story of your life?*

3. *Jesus ended the enmity between God and you. He removed your guilt and paid the price for your sin. Spend a few moments contemplating this.*

4. *In what way does God's word of comfort free you from the past? How does it free you to embrace tomorrow?*

The presence
of God
is our goal

*A voice cries: "In the wilderness prepare the way of the LORD; make straight in the desert a highway for our God.*

*"Every valley shall be lifted up, and every mountain and hill be made low; the uneven ground shall become level, and the rough places a plain.*

*"And the glory of the LORD shall be revealed, and all flesh shall see it together, for the mouth of the LORD has spoken."*

*A voice says, "Cry!" And I said, "What shall I cry?" All flesh is grass, and all its beauty is like the flower of the field.*

*"The grass withers, the flower fades when the breath of the LORD blows on it; surely the people are grass.*

*"The grass withers, the flower fades, but the word of our God will stand forever."*

*Isaiah 40:3–8*

We have so much, yet we possess so little. We have Bible translations galore, yet we understand so little. We have study materials of every variety, yet pursue the Word of God so little. We possess Christian books and literature unlike any other generation in the history of the world. We have choices and options for worship and local church involvement that stagger the imagination. We can go to gospel concerts with lights, promotion, presence, staging, choreography, multimedia, and pizzazz to rival any secular production. The Yellow Pages lists Christian lawyers, plumbers, doctors, and electricians. We have so much, yet we seem to possess so little. Something is missing—something vital.

Israel of old could have commiserated with us, for she too

knew something was missing. Something was gone, something whose absence made all else seem hollow, cheap, gaudy, and lifeless. That something was the glory of God in her midst. It is this that we also are too often devoid of.

Ezekiel had been entrusted with the burden of seeing God's glory recede from the temple and depart into the wilderness.[1] The Ichabod-nation was left with religious forms, traditions, memories, and nostalgia, but little else. Look around at what passes for Christianity—are we any better?

We must have the glory of the Lord in our midst again. The glory of God is our goal. Isaiah told us so: "the glory of the LORD shall be revealed" (40:5a). Oh, what hope that brings! So thirsty for his glorious presence are we that our breath grows shallow and rapid at even the hint that it could be true. Could we actually experience his glory in our midst? Do we dare believe it could be so?

Yes. Absolutely, yes! This has been the longing of God's people throughout all generations. It is our God-given goal. Isaiah tells us how we can see God's glory revealed in us.

> A voice cries: "In the wilderness prepare the way of the
>    LORD;
>   make straight in the desert a highway for our God.
> Every valley shall be lifted up,
>    and every mountain and hill be made low;
> the uneven ground shall become level,
>    and the rough places a plain."

(vv. 3–4)

Isaiah's words describe the ancient practice of preparing a processional way for the grand arrival of a king. It was into the wilderness that Ezekiel would watch the glory of God go. It is now "In the wilderness" that the way must be prepared for God's glorious presence to return to the midst of his people. His people must "make straight" the winding, crooked way "in the desert." "Every valley" is to be filled in and brought up to level so that the King's passage is dignified and proper. Every "mountain and hill" is to be leveled and every obstruction removed. The grading and preparation are to be so thorough that "the uneven ground shall become level, and the rough places a plain."

All this bespeaks an intense and intentional preparation in anticipation of the return of God's glory to our midst. But what is the reality behind these metaphors? What are the preparations we must make if we are to be the dwelling place of God's glorious presence? In a word, *repentance*.

These words of Isaiah (vv. 3–5) are quoted in all four Gospels as having been fulfilled in the ministry of John the Baptist.[2] John's message was simple: "Repent, for the kingdom of heaven is at hand" (Matt. 3:2). As God draws near, he longs to manifest his glorious presence in his people. Repentance is the human preparation for that grand revelation on the altar of our lives.

When we get serious about repentance, God will gloriously make himself known in us. And not until. When this is true,

"*Then* the glory of the LORD will be revealed" (Isa. 40:5a, NASB, emphasis added).

Isaiah's words were fulfilled in Jesus. "And the Word became flesh and dwelt among us, and we have seen his glory, glory as of the only Son from the Father, full of grace and truth" (John 1:14). "He is the radiance of the glory of God and the exact imprint of his nature" (Heb. 1:3a). "For God, who said, 'Let light shine out of darkness,' has shone in our hearts to give the light of the knowledge of the glory of God in the face of Jesus Christ" (2 Cor. 4:6).

When God the Son took on a human nature and body and entered the human race, God was manifesting his glory. *As Jesus lived out his earthly pilgrimage* he was manifesting the glory of God: "I glorified you on earth, having accomplished the work that you gave me to do" (John 17:4). *When Jesus died*, he was manifesting the glory of God: "The hour has come for the Son of Man to be glorified. Truly, truly, I say to you, unless a grain of wheat falls into the earth and dies, it remains alone; but if it dies, it bears much fruit'" (John 12:23–24). Jesus manifested the glory of God *when he rose from the dead*: "Christ was raised from the dead by the glory of the Father" (Rom. 6:4). *When Jesus ascended to heaven and was seated at the Father's right hand* he was manifesting the glory of God. Stephen, as he died, "gazed into heaven and saw the glory of God, and Jesus standing at the right hand of God" (Acts 7:55). Indeed, "Isaiah said these things because he saw his glory and spoke of him" (John 12:41).

God *has done* this. God *did* reveal his glory in Christ and his redemptive work. But there is more. God's glory longs for a continuing manifestation. And it has everything to do with you and me. God has "called you to his eternal glory in Christ" (1 Peter 5:10).

Christ longs to come again to his temple and make his glory burn in manifest splendor. You personally are that temple (1 Cor. 6:19). We, collectively as the people of God, are that temple (1 Cor. 3:16). The glory of God is our calling and, therefore, also our goal.

> Lift up your heads, O gates!
>  And be lifted up, O ancient doors,
>   that the King of glory may come in.
> Who is this King of glory?
>  The LORD, strong and mighty,
>   the LORD, mighty in battle!
> Lift up your heads, O gates!
>  And lift them up, O ancient doors,
>   that the King of glory may come in.
> Who is this King of glory?
>  The LORD of hosts,
>   he is the King of glory!
>
> (Ps. 24:7–10)

Does Christ dwell gloriously within the temple of your body, manifesting himself upon the altar of your heart through the sacrifice of your obedience? Does he make known his glorious presence as he dwells within the local assembly of believers where you worship?

These questions unsettle us. What would such a manifestation look like? How would it appear? What would others see in and among us when it took place?

Luke made a subtle but significant change when he quoted Isaiah 40:3–5 in reference to the ministry of John the Baptist. Where Isaiah had said, "the *glory* of the LORD shall be revealed, and all flesh shall see it together," (v. 5), Luke wrote, "all flesh shall see the *salvation* of God" (Luke 3:6, emphasis added). Do you see? The salvation you enjoy is to become the grandest demonstration of the glory of God known among mankind. Martyn Lloyd-Jones put it this way: "The supreme manifestation of this glory is in the salvation which the Son has brought."[3]

Our entire existence and calling as believers is wrapped up in the pursuit of the manifestation of the glorious God in our lives: "And we all, with unveiled face, beholding the glory of the Lord, are being transformed into the same image from one degree of glory to another" (2 Cor. 3:18a). We are caught up with beholding the glorious Person of Christ. And we are thus caught up in the blessed process of being transformed into his likeness—"from one degree of glory to another." And all this "comes from the Lord who is the Spirit" dwelling gloriously within us (v. 18b). This glorious God—preeminent over all the earth, all the nations, all the idols, all the rulers, and all the heavens—is committed to ever-increasingly making himself seen in your life!

Can this be? Will this be? Yes, as we *repent*. And not until. If the glory of God is our goal, the steps toward that goal require dealing seriously with the obstacles that impede his glorious manifestation of himself in us. Our greatest blunder resides here: "all have sinned and fall short of the glory of God" (Rom. 3:23). Our greatest honor is to "do all to the glory of God" (1 Cor. 10:31b). If we prepare, he will come. If we clean the house, he will dwell within it.

It is his guarantee: "for the mouth of the LORD has spoken" (Isa. 40:5b). Is his word good? Nothing is more certain.

> A voice says, "Cry!"
>   And I said, "What shall I cry?"
> All flesh is grass,
>   and all its beauty is like the flower of the field.
> The grass withers, the flower fades
>   when the breath of the LORD blows on it;
>   surely the people are grass.
> The grass withers, the flower fades,
>   but the word of our God will stand forever.
>
> (vv. 6–8)

The glory of God is our greatest hope, for the process he works in us now will be fully and finally completed at Christ's return (Rom. 8:30). All that is human will wither and tumble away in the breeze, but God's Word will prove true. Nothing we experience now is "worth comparing with the glory that is to be revealed to us" (Rom. 8:18). One thing about tomorrow is absolutely certain: Whatever it may hold, it can be made to contribute to the manifest presence of Christ in our lives—now and in eternity.

### Reflect on these points

*1. Is there any perplexity that a fresh perception of God in his glory wouldn't solve?*

*2. When we get serious about repentance, God will gloriously make himself known to us. Ask God if you have any unfinished business in this regard.*

*3. Your entire existence and calling as a believer is wrapped up in the pursuit of the manifestation of the glorious God in your life. Do you heartily share this goal with God?*

*4. Tomorrow—whatever it may bring—can be made to contribute to the manifest presence of Christ in your life. How does this knowledge promote peace within you?*

The presence
of God is
our confidence

*Behold, the Lord GOD comes with might, and his arm rules for him; behold, his reward is with him, and his recompense before him.*

*He will tend his flock like a shepherd; he will gather the lambs in his arms; he will carry them in his bosom, and gently lead those that are with young.*

*Isaiah 40:10–11*

Have you ever tried to point out a star to a preschooler? Not just any star, but a particular one? It's not easy to do. I tried once to point out the Big Dipper to my preschool-aged son. I kept saying, "There! It's right there!" All the while I was pointing in animated fashion toward the sky. He stared into the darkness with a blank expression on his face. I described the stars around it: "See that big one there? It's just over that way a little from there?" Nope. I brought him in near my side, his head pressed up against mine so his eyes could be as near mine as possible. I tried guiding his eyes up my arm, past my elbow, down my pointing finger … "See? See it? It's right there!" "Where, Daddy?" Argh!

He was just too preoccupied with the world at hand. He could not see more than a few yards beyond the end of my finger. The stellar landscape was just not within his worldview yet. No amount of explanation, animation, or declaration could make his eyes take it in. Yet the star was very definitely *there*.

Not dissimilar was the time I tried to point out to him a small rainbow created over a waterfall we were beholding. "Oh, look! It's a rainbow!" I exclaimed. "What? Where?" "There! Right there over the mist rising from the waterfall!" You know the routine—pointed fingers, extended explanations, animated gestures. Nope. Not going to happen. He knew rainbows appear in the sky, not within a few yards of where you are standing. He kept looking *through* the mist, not *at* it. He was just too caught up with the world beyond. He was taken up with the hard realities of rocks, trees, and earth—no amount of pointing and pronouncing was going to make him see. Yet the rainbow was *there*. Really, it was.

Isaiah has been calling us to *see*. He is so exercised in his desire for us to perceive what he perceives that he repeats himself three times in rapid succession: "Behold ... Behold ... behold" (vv. 9–10). Can you see his animated gestures and the exercised expression upon his face? Can you hear the urgency in his voice? There is something we simply must *see*! Or, more accurately, Someone.

Isaiah now reveals just exactly who it is he sees and why we need so desperately to see him too. If you can get the lenses of faith in place, you will see that God is drawing near you in a twofold role. He is approaching as both a warrior King (v. 10) and a gentle Shepherd (v. 11). He draws near as both tough and tender.

Look! This *warrior King* draws near! "Behold, the Lord GOD comes with might." He is *Adonai-Yahweh*—the covenant God and our sovereign Master. And as he approaches we see that he "comes with might," or more literally "comes as a

Strong One." The exact form of the word is used elsewhere only of God's "strong hand" extended in miraculous power to bring his people out of slavery to Pharaoh and Egypt (Exod. 13:3, 14, 16). Here too he comes as a Deliverer. Nothing that restricts you from doing his will is safe in his presence. He comes to liberate you and set you free to run the path of his commands.

And look, "his arm rules for him." The Bible often speaks of God's outstretched arm as a symbol of his ruling power. Our God comes as a King, for his arm "*rules* for him." He comes as a victorious Warrior, for he advances as the "Strong One." Where God's arm is extended, no opposition stands. No foe can sweep it away. When God rules by his arm, his kingdom comes and his will is done. Period.

And behold, "his reward is with him, and his recompense before him"! The word "reward" was used of the wages paid a servant, soldier, or shepherd. Then it came to describe, more broadly, a reward for any work faithfully completed. Similarly, the word "recompense" spoke of wages paid for such labor. What are these wages our God has earned? It is *you*! And all the other redeemed of the Lord. "You were bought with a price" (1 Cor. 7:23). It is "the church of God, which he obtained with his own blood" (Acts 20:28). Indeed, the song that fills heaven's halls is "Worthy are you ... for you were slain, and by your blood you ransomed people for God from every tribe and language and people and nation" (Rev. 5:9).

The warrior King has conquered! He has conquered you. He has conquered your former taskmaster. He has utterly defeated every foe that might ever threaten you. Such raw power and authority might frighten, were it not for the fact that this universal victory was secured at the cost of his life's blood. There is a heart of compassion driving this arm of strength.

Indeed, the same God who approaches as the warrior King at one and the same time draws near as the *gentle Shepherd* (Isa. 40:11). He is not only a Being of infinite power and unrivaled authority, but he is also gracious and tender, dealing with his people as "his flock" and caring for them "like a shepherd." Imagine! Infinite power, unrivaled authority, undiluted insight—all committed to your personal welfare!

Look! "He will tend his flock like a shepherd." He feeds and leads. He cares and spares. He heals and helps. He dotes over you as one of his own. "I am the good shepherd. I know my own and my own know me" (John 10:14). With all the insight of infinite knowledge and wisdom, he assesses your life, your needs, and your desires, and then tends you with love.

As Shepherd, "he will gather the lambs in his arms." Note that the arm that rules with sovereign, miraculous power (v. 10) is the arm that gently, lovingly gathers his own to his side (v. 11). It was, as Isaiah prophetically saw it, the arm of the Lord that would redeem us from our sin. "And to whom has the arm of the LORD been revealed?" (53:1b). Answer? It is to you and to me, who have heard the gospel of Jesus! His strong, gentle arm of redeeming love has, through that gospel message, extended to us and sought to draw us into his grace. Jesus, the Good Shepherd, still tells us, "And I have other sheep that are not of this fold. I must bring them also, and they will listen to my voice. So there will be one flock, one shepherd" (John 10:16).

Having gathered up his own, "he will carry them in his bosom." This is an expression of the deepest intimacy and safety. "My sheep hear my voice, and I know them, and they follow me" (John 10:27). No relationship could be safer. "The eternal God is your dwelling place, and underneath are the everlasting arms" (Deut. 33:27a).

He knows our frame and what we can stand. He recognizes those which are but "lambs"—the young, immature, and most vulnerable. He knows "those that are with young"—referring not to the pregnant, but to those with small lambs still nursing at their mother's side. He gives special attention and care to each according to their needs. "God is faithful, and he will not let you be tempted beyond your ability" (1 Cor. 10:13).

Our Shepherd does not stand behind the sheep and drive them, but he will "gently lead" them. Every step he calls you to, he has already walked before you arrive there—"we do not have a high priest who is unable to sympathize with our weaknesses, but one who in every respect has been tempted as we are, yet without sin" (Heb. 4:15). He has gone before, stands ahead, and motions you forward—to himself. He is the destination to which you are being called. He will not leave before you approach and he will not depart once you arrive.

He leads you. And he does so "gently." The arm of omnipotent power is under the controlling influence of infinite love.

With such a God, does not tomorrow somehow look more doable? Isn't there a new confidence about stepping into the shadowy unknown of what will be, just knowing Who is already there?

Do you *see*? Can you *behold* that this preeminent God draws near you now as the warrior King and gentle Shepherd? Some are too caught up with *the world at hand* to see the God beyond who draws near them. Others are too caught up with *the world beyond* to see the simple evidences that God has come near. "I pray that your hearts will be flooded with light so that you can understand the confident hope he has given to those he called— his holy people who are his rich and glorious inheritance" (Eph. 1:18, NLT).

### Reflect on these points

*1. God draws near to you as a warrior King. What does this mean for you today?*

*2. Nothing that restricts you from doing God's will is safe in his presence.*

*3. God comes to you as a gentle Shepherd. There is a heart of compassion driving the arm of his omnipotence.*

*4. Your Shepherd leads you. He goes before you and invites you to himself. How does this help you face tomorrow?*

# The presence
of God
is our hope

*Why do you say, O Jacob, and speak, O Israel, "My way is hidden from the LORD, and my right is disregarded by my God"?*

*Have you not known? Have you not heard? The LORD is the everlasting God, the Creator of the ends of the earth. He does not faint or grow weary; his understanding is unsearchable.*

*Isaiah 40:27–28*

*It's not fair!* I've heard it from my kids, from co-workers, from church people, and from various assorted strangers worked up enough to confide in me. And yes, I've also heard it echoing in my own heart and rolling off my own lips. We've all felt we've gotten a rotten deal. And we're not afraid to say so.

In time we often realize that, even if the sting of injustice remains, many of the issues were really not that big a deal. Small potatoes compared with what some folk face. But injustice—when it is yours—smarts, whatever the issues. Complaining, griping, carping, moaning, and grousing all seem legitimate responses.

Certainly Israel, after decades in foreign exile, would find herself tempted with such bitter reflection. So the prophet, anticipating such a response, asks, "Why do you say, O Jacob, and speak, O Israel, 'My way is hidden from the LORD, and my right is disregarded by my God'?"

We often *think* we have received an unfair verdict—at the hands of our bosses, friends, family, church leaders, or others. But frequently we are able to process through to a place of resolution in our hearts concerning these matters. There are other times, however, when the desired rest never seems to arrive and our thoughts become words of complaint. Israel was articulating her contentions: "Why do you *say*, O Jacob, and *speak*, O Israel …?" Inward doubts had become open, defiant demands for an answer from God. And they were coming from "Jacob" and "Israel." "Let them remember," says Matthew Henry, "whence they took these names—from one who had found God faithful to him and kind in all his straits; and why they bore these names—as God's professing people, a people in covenant with him."[1] All the worse! Being the covenant people only raised their expectations of God. And now *this*!

Their complaint took two forms. First, "My way is hidden from the LORD." The word "way" is a figurative expression to describe the course of one's life—the path one walks on this journey through life. This, they were saying, was "hidden" from God. The Hebrew verb is used figuratively to describe something that seems to have escaped God's notice. Second, they were saying, "my right is disregarded by my God." The word translated "my right" is the Hebrew expression for justice. Here it has the notion of judgment.[2] The verdict that had allowed their current circumstances did not appear just. They believed they deserved better. They believed God's covenant guaranteed them something better. But, in their view, their right had been "disregarded." The verb means to "pass over." God was too preoccupied with other matters and had simply passed over the "right" that was due them. As if God is incapable of multitasking!

Note the purposeful juxtaposition of terms: "my right ... my God." Their conclusion was, "*My rights* are not safe in the hands of *my God*!" Ever felt that way? Then perhaps you've been making the same mistake they made—the mistake of measuring God from your circumstances rather than your circumstances from God. It does matter where you place the end of the tape measure. It matters because it reveals something about your basic orientation to life. Are my circumstances to be measured by the objective standard of God's nature? Or is God to be evaluated by the nature of my circumstances?

At such moments we are forgetting something basic. Isaiah asks, "Have you not known? Have you not heard?" These are the same two questions that were asked in verse 21, but the tense of the verbs has changed. There the imperfect tense pointed to ongoing action without reference to its completion. They should have been coming into the knowledge that God was different from how they had thought him to be. Here, however, the verbs are in the perfect tense—pointing to what should have been completed action. By now they should have come to know God better than this![3] But, alas, too often we must relearn what we should have already known. Thus Isaiah helpfully reminds us of ground already covered—ground upon which we leverage ourselves against the cancer of complaints.

*God is not bound by time*—for he "is the everlasting God." He existed before "the beginning" and has been revealing himself "from the foundations of the earth" (v. 21). Time is one of God's creations—like space, energy, and mass. He resides outside of time and engulfs it in his own eternal Person. He is not subject to the progression of advancing moments nor does he experience things in a succession of events as we time-bound creatures do. His seeing, knowing, and governing of all the events of his creation take place from a vantage point outside of time.

*God is not bound by space*—for he is "the Creator of the ends of the earth." "Lift up your eyes on high and see: who created these?" (v. 26a). Indeed, God "is he who sits above the circle of the earth, and its inhabitants are like grasshoppers" (v. 22a). God is immense, filling every portion of his creation. He is omnipresent—present in the fullness of his Person at every point in his creation. God not only fills all of creation, but he also engulfs all of his creation, transcending all spatial limitations. God does not dwell in space, rather space dwells in him. "Remember that God is outside of all things and inside of all things and around all things."[4] God does not have to "come" to us. He does not have to race to our aid. He is ever accessible—instantly, immediately present at all points in his creation.

*God is not bound in power*—for "He does not faint or grow weary." He "comes with might, and his arm rules for him" (v. 10a). "[B]y the greatness of his might, and because he is strong in power not one [star or planet] is missing" (v. 26b). God can do anything he wills to do. I must remember that God's power does not exist for my purposes, but for his. I must be thankful that, though God can do all he wills, he will not do all he can. I must never lose sight of the fact that sometimes God's power is best seen in what he will not do, rather than what he could do.

*God is not bound in knowledge*—for "his understanding is unsearchable." The word "understanding" has reference to discerning between things. God is not simply a database of infinite information but a discerning, wise God with an all-encompassing knowledge of all things. God's understanding "is unsearchable." Theologians refer to this as God's inscrutability. God is beyond knowing in his fullness. He is knowable and personal and in his grace reveals himself to us, yet God is ultimately an "unsearchable" mystery and beyond knowing exhaustively. God is not an encyclopedia to be searched, but a Person to be known, albeit only on his terms. We will spend eternity discovering who he is—and some of all he knows. "Whom did he consult, and who made him understand? Who taught him the path of justice, and taught him knowledge, and showed him the way of understanding?" (v. 14).

God is not bound. He is free, unfettered, unrestricted. Nothing binds God. Yet there is one thing (and only one thing) that binds God—his own nature. He is "The LORD"—Yahweh, the covenant-making, covenant-keeping God of grace. Only the self-imposed restriction of his covenant promises made to us puts any limitation upon God. Only his nature as a faithful, covenant-keeping God limits him. Only his gracious promises, made out of no obligation on his part, restrict him in any way. God is completely free, unfettered, unhindered, unobstructed.

He can do as he pleases, and all that he pleases is done. Nothing can stop his hand. Nothing can ultimately resist his will. Yet he has set his pleasure upon keeping a Bible full of promises to his covenant people. He commits his will and all his infinite resources to fulfilling what he has spoken to you.

His covenant Name had been on the lips of his people ("My way is hidden from *the* LORD"), but he had not filled the horizon of their hearts. They had placed the tape measure at the wrong end and were measuring God by their circumstances.

What time, space, power, and information cannot do, God's own divine nature does. It binds him—to his covenant promises to you. God is just. Justice will be done. There can be no other outcome. God is not bound by time—justice comes at his pace. We often do not understand that time, but we can rest assured that no statute of limitations will restrict God from exacting justice for every wrong done. God is not bound by space, so there is no place to which a culprit can flee and be beyond the arm of his justice. God is not bound in power, so nothing can block the inevitable justice he must work against all unrighteousness. God is not bound in knowledge. He knows everything. *Everything!* All the unseen acts, all the injustices thought to be covered and whose tracks have been erased. There is no "perfect crime" against God.

The preeminent God is just. He sees. He knows. He owns tomorrow. He will bring justice. He can and will do no other. Rest your case with God. Leave your hurts with him.

Reflect on these points

1. *In what way are you tempted to conclude that God has not been just in his dealings with you?*

2. *How have you been measuring God by your circumstances rather than measuring your circumstances by God?*

3. *How does knowing that God is not bound by time, space, power, or knowledge assure you of justice in his dealings with you?*

4. *What is the one thing that binds God? How does this nurture courage and peace within you?*

The presence
of God is
our strength

*He gives power to the faint, and to him who has no might he increases strength.*

*Even youths shall faint and be weary, and young men shall fall exhausted;*

*but they who wait for the LORD shall renew their strength; they shall mount up with wings like eagles; they shall run and not be weary; they shall walk and not faint.*

*Isaiah 40:29–31*

*I can't.* It was all I could do to form the words. I was face down in the cold, damp mud, wearing nothing but a light pair of shorts and a tank top. Standing over me, having issued the order "Get up!" was my high-school track coach. I had just finished running a quarter of a mile as fast as I possibly could. I had received the baton from my relay teammate about one stride behind the lead runner. I determined I would not allow him to distance himself from me. I was not normally a quarter-miler. I usually competed in shorter races like the 100 or 220 yards. This longest of the sprints tested the limits of my endurance and my resolve. The other runner was one of his team's best racers at this distance. One lap later I had not surrendered one inch … nor had I gained one. I'd given it all I had. I left it all on the track. Having passed the baton to the next runner, I managed to half fall into the infield and land face down in the wet grass on that raw, windy spring day. It was over. That was it. Not only was the race finished, *I* was finished.

*I can't.* Too often it's a lame excuse. We really mean "I won't" or "I don't want to," but we know those don't sell as well. Sometimes, however, everything within us believes it is true. I simply can't.

All we've heard and seen of God in Isaiah 40 is wonderful, but what happens when at the end of the day I simply cannot lift my foot for another step? What about the times when "I can't" isn't a cliché or a cover-up, but a stark, honest confession? We have all come to the end of ourselves and had to face the terror of tomorrow's demands. We *must* all come to that place. Yes, *must.* Must, that is, if we are ever to enter into the strength of the Lord. In fact, many of his dealings with us are designed to bring us to this end.

Isaiah 40 appropriately comes to an end by bringing us to the end of our strength. For at our end is a glorious new beginning. At the end of ourselves is the beginning of his strength. If you are "faint and weary" and are about to "fall exhausted," you are on the right path. It is not a sign you have lost your way, but that you are on his way. It happens to all of us, even the best of us and even in our prime—"Even youths shall faint and be weary, and young men shall fall exhausted" (v. 30).

If you are tired of the race and weary of the pace—you are in the right place. For "He gives power to the faint, and to him who has no might he increases strength" (v. 29). Now here's good news! And Isaiah delivers it by picking up on several key words from his earlier description of the preeminent God. The very struggle that identifies us ("the faint," v. 29) is a problem foreign to God ("He does not faint," v. 28). The arena of our greatest problem ("has no might," v. 29) is the venue of God's greatest power ("the greatness of his might" holds stars and planets in space, v. 26). We may be "weary" (v. 30), but "He does not ... grow weary" (v. 28). Do you hear how good this news is? The very thing in which we are failing is precisely that in which God excels! He is perfect where we are imperfect—in the arena of power, strength, and might.

God's intention is to make his strength your strength. He who is completely unfettered—unhindered by time, space, energy, or knowledge (v. 28)—intends to infuse you with his might. How does God make his strength our strength? There are only two prerequisites. The first is simply this: *Weariness.* "Now *that* I can do," you may be thinking. Indulge yourself in the thought, for it's from God. Little wonder the apostle Paul declares, "I will boast all the more gladly of my weaknesses, so that the power of Christ may rest upon me ... For when I am weak, then I am strong" (2 Cor. 12:9–10). We've got this prerequisite covered. No homework to do here.

The second prerequisite is this: *Waiting.* This looks a little tougher. Look more closely at what Isaiah is saying. The Hebrew word translated "wait" in Isaiah 40:31 combines the ideas of waiting and hoping. It is not just waiting, but waiting with expectation. We've got more than enough experience in waiting without hope. Doctors' offices, traffic jams, and being put on hold have taught us plenty about how to wait without hope. We need to figure out how to wait in hope—confident, expectant hope.

An alternate translation for "wait" is "look for." The word may well come from a root meaning to twist or stretch[1]— we might describe it as craning the neck so we can *see*. This brings us back to the key to the whole chapter and the key to tomorrow—"Behold your God!" (v. 9).

We watchfully *wait* upon the Lord because we've come to the end of ourselves and we know the next step is impossible apart from his strength. We watchfully *hope* in the Lord because he is just that—"the LORD." He is Yahweh, the covenant God of love and faithfulness. In his love he has committed himself to us in a vast array of promises contained in the Scriptures. In his faithfulness he keeps every one. Because we have seen him to be preeminent, our souls are convinced that waiting upon him is no risk. This waiting in expectant hope is at one and the same time passive and active. It is passive in that we know we can't do God's will on our own and there is nothing to be done but to wait for his provision of strength. It is active in that we obediently move forward in his will with the confidence that, when we take up his will—and not before—we receive his power.

When weary people come to grips with their powerlessness and wait in hope upon the covenant God of all power, a remarkable process begins to take place. In this process the Lord "gives" and "increases" (v. 29), and "renew[s]" (v. 31). This last term is used in this verbal form to describe changing one's clothes (e.g. Gen. 35:2; Ps. 102:26). It can also have the sense of substituting or exchanging one thing for another.[2] As you wait in active confidence upon the Lord you are shedding the garments of weakness and being clothed with power (Luke 24:49). As you wait upon the Lord you are trading in your inability for his infinite ability. The verbal tense suggests this is an ongoing, unending process—as long as you actively, obediently wait, the flow of power will never dry up.

That process of exchange is beautifully gathered up in a graphic word picture: "they shall mount up with wings like eagles." The verb means simply to go up or to ascend. And how is this achieved? Not with mighty thrashing of the wings, but by simply extending those pinions and exposing them to another power. The eagle rides the mighty updrafts of wind for hours without ever flapping its wings. An eagle in flight is majestic, but its majesty resides not in its inherent strength, but in its ability to be lifted by an even greater power.

Such flight appears effortless, but it is not a naturally acquired skill. Moses pictured the terrifying process the eaglet must endure in order to learn to soar upon the heights. Metaphorically speaking of his dealings with Israel, God said, "Like an eagle that stirs up its nest, that flutters over its young, spreading out its wings, catching them, bearing them on its pinions, the LORD alone guided him, no foreign god was with him" (Deut. 32:11–12). The eagle "stirs up its nest" by thrusting the young eaglet from the safety of solid ground and into thin air. Unable to take flight by any expenditure of effort, the eaglet plunges downward. The mother eagle swoops beneath and catches her young upon her back, placing it back again in the safety of the nest. Repeating the process regularly, the mother aids the growing eaglet to eventually discover that flight is not a matter of trying harder, but of trusting more fully in the power of the wind. Soon enough, the young eagle is riding the breezes and rising to new heights. It is an amazing sight. Indeed, Solomon said, "Three things are too wonderful for me; four I do not understand," and the first one he named was "the way of an eagle in the sky" (Prov. 30:18–19). Similarly, our steps of obedience pick up the wind of God's Spirit and we are enabled to rise to heights previously unknown and unknowable in our own strength.

The picture is brought to our turf by the words, "they shall run and not be weary; they shall walk and not faint." To expend oneself in an activity like running or walking and yet never grow tired would require an "in-flight" renewal process—somehow restoring the energy being expended even while continuing the activity by which the energy is being spent. This is precisely what God promises here to do for us. As we obey, he replaces our strength with his. As we continue to obey, he continues the transfer of divine strength to our human hearts, minds, and frames. The result is a constant inner renewal, even while outwardly expending tremendous amounts of energy. Here is the secret of divine fellowship: For every step of obedience there is an immediate and commensurate inflow of divine enablement. It is not a contradiction to speak of waiting upon the Lord and in the same breath to talk of running or walking. Waiting on the Lord is not a matter of inactivity, but of obedience. We wait upon the Lord as we obey, not knowing how we can, but trusting (waiting) that as we do so, his strength will be given and we will be enabled in the step of obedience we have undertaken. In obedience we launch from the nest without the inherent strength to do anything but fall, but, as we dutifully spread our wings in obedience, his Spirit lifts and enables us in the matter before us.

The only way we will ever "wait for the LORD" is if we first "Behold [our] God" (v. 9). He must become our occupation. We must look upon our God, studying him in his preeminence. Then, and only then, will we wait upon him in obedience and have the reasonable hope that he will prove in our experience to be exactly who he declares himself to be.

## Reflect on these points

1. *Why does God work to bring you to the end of yourself? Why is this a necessary work? How has he been bringing this about in you?*

2. *How does God make his strength your strength? Are you meeting his requirements for this transfer to take place?*

3. *What does waiting in hope look like in your life? How is that a passive matter? In what way must it be active?*

4. *Waiting on the Lord is not a matter of inactivity, but of obedience. What does this require of you today?*

# The peace of God

*"Behold, I will extend peace to her like a river."*

**Isaiah 66:12a**

Not far to the east of where I live the Allegheny and Monongahela Rivers converge upon a singular meeting point. Having gathered in countless rivulets, brooks, streams, and rivers, these waters meandered along, collecting into ever-increasingly larger bodies of water. Never resting, always flowing, these waters search out the ultimate expression of their collective power. The resulting confluence is the mighty Ohio River. The Ohio River would not exist without the Allegheny and Monongahela Rivers. The Allegheny and Monongahela find their fulfillment in the power of the Ohio's swift current. Their waters flow toward a convergence, and they not only clash in a powerful confluence, but they also make an even more awesome emergence into something that would not otherwise have existed.

Where there is a convergence of the preeminence and presence of God, there is then a confluence that flows away in a single powerful torrent made up of both. That confluence can never be entered if there is not first the convergence of the preeminence and presence of God. What does one call the comfort, purpose, confidence, hope, and strength that flow from the manifest presence of the One completely preeminent over all things and yet lovingly committed to one's welfare? The single word that gathers all that up and puts expression to it is *peace*.

If God is deemed near but is not exalted for who he truly is, peace is forfeited and a chummy but impotent folk-god is left awaiting our embrace. If God is exalted as transcendent above all but is not deemed to be immanent, peace is forfeited and a stern dictator stands over us. A weak sense of goodwill is all the one can deliver, and the other a quaking fear. But where the preeminence of God is established and the presence of God is manifested, there the God of peace is embraced and the peace of God emerges.

Many people want to emerge into the peace of God. Too many of them, however, are not willing to make the personal, spiritual journey to the place of convergence between the preeminence and presence of God. Even if they are, they too often arrive as mere spiritual sightseers and are unwilling to dive into the churning, rushing confluence they find. Thus they never make the longed-for emergence into the peace of God.

Convergence, confluence, emergence—it is an inviolable spiritual pattern which takes shape from the text of Isaiah's prophecy.

It's so simple. *Right?*

Simple, yes. Simplistic, no. Why is it we don't experience more peace? We worship, we pray, we read, we seek. Why, then, so little peace within? The reason why we do not experience peace is because the threats we face are bigger than the gods we serve. The objects of our worship are no match for the obstacles we face. Most of us worry and fret because we believe we need smaller problems. That is, after all, why we enlist the help of our gods—to diminish our problems. However, the answer to peace is not found in smaller problems, but in serving a bigger God.

This is precisely why the order of God's spiritual pattern must be maintained—first the preeminence of God, then the presence of God, resulting in the peace of God. We seek peace from a diminished god and wonder why we feel so alone and lack rest in our souls. When God is apprehended and appreciated for who he is, his presence is manifested, our problems are put in perspective—and peace is the inevitable result.

We must do business with "the God of peace" before we can experience "the peace of God" (Phil. 4:7, 9). Indeed, Paul prayed, "Now may *the Lord of peace* himself *give you peace* at all times in every way" (2 Thes. 3:16a, emphasis added).

How did God answer the apostle's prayer? And how does he answer still?

"The God of peace" sent his Son to remove the enmity created by our sins. He did this through his sacrificial and substitutionary death upon the cross. God's preeminent holiness and justice demanded peace be made in the war which we began through our rebellion (Eph. 2:1–3). Remember, Isaiah twice said, "There is no peace ... for the wicked" (Isa. 48:22; 57:21). Jesus was "making peace by the blood of his cross" (Col. 1:20). This is "peace with God" (Rom. 5:1). The God of peace, through his Son Jesus Christ, first established peace *with* God so that we might be able to live evermore in the peace *of* God. Peace *with* God is a settled fact resting upon the completed and perfect work of Jesus Christ. It is a *fact* to be believed, not a work yet to be done. The peace *of* God is a subjective *experience* that flows out of Christ's completed work and into the heart which has established itself through faith on that finished work. "Peace with God" is something we enter through firm belief; the "peace of God" is something we experience in an ongoing life of trusting obedience.

Jesus Christ is the One Isaiah prophesied as the coming "Prince of Peace" (Isa. 9:6). Isaiah's contemporary and fellow-prophet, Micah, said of Christ, "This One will be our peace" (Micah 5:5a, NASB). As Jesus prepared to leave his followers, he comforted them, saying, "Peace I leave with you; my peace I give to you. Not as the world gives do I give to you. Let not your hearts be troubled, neither let them be afraid" (John 14:27).

It is in the Person of Jesus Christ that the preeminent God has manifested himself for the purposes of making peace with mankind (John 1:14, 18). It is in Jesus that the preeminence and presence of God converge as "the God of peace." The confluence of those two streams is the resulting "peace with God" (Rom. 5:1). The life that emerges is full of "the peace of God" (Phil. 4:7).

These truths must be embraced in personal trust before they become our experience. The resurrection of Jesus Christ assured us not only that his provision for sin was sufficient, but also that the enjoyment of the resulting life can be personal. Jesus lives! He longs to live his life in you. As you open the door to an ever-deepening life of relationship to Christ (Rev. 3:20), your life becomes the point of convergence for these realities. In you the preeminent God begins to manifest his presence, and the confluence of peace *with* God begins to ever-increasingly emerge into a life characterized by the peace *of* God.

Is all this river-talk just word-picture and metaphor? Yes, but it is *God's* metaphor, spoken through Isaiah and pointing to a firm reality. As he sealed his prophecy with the promise of perfect, eternal peace, Isaiah declared, "For thus says the LORD: 'Behold, I will extend peace to her *like a river*'" (Isa. 66:12, emphasis added).

A river can be enjoyed in one of two ways: as a tourist or as a traveler. The first requires little, and, frankly, it results in little. It demands no more than that you dawdle along its banks, gawking at its beauty. As a tourist you'll want to dangle a toe in the water, but you'll never actually enter the river. The second demands a good deal more—surrender to the current, direction, and power of the river. This price is higher, but it results in an entirely new life.

Indeed, this offer is God's parting word to us as the last page of Scripture is turned: "Then the angel showed me the river of the water of life, bright as crystal, flowing from the throne of God and of the Lamb … The Spirit and the Bride say, 'Come.' And let the one who hears say, 'Come.' And let the one who is thirsty come; let the one who desires take the water of life without price" (Rev. 22:1, 17).

Tomorrow need not be a terrifying tyrant. Difficult though it may be, it can be embraced as a friend. As a word, "tomorrow" may indeed be the most uncertain in our language, but as an experience it may become the springboard that sends you deep into the life of God, surging with strong currents of peace and swift rapids of grace. All that is required is that you surrender to the current of the river of God's Life, flowing down from the throne of God and cutting a chasm directly through the regions of your heart.

Because God is God, tomorrow can be a new day. Because God is who he says he is and has done what he says he has done, you can enter tomorrow as a new person, living a new life. All God asks is that you "Come" in simple, surrendered, trusting faith. When you do, you will find that ...

> Like a river glorious is God's perfect peace,
> Over all victorious, in its bright increase;
> Perfect, yet it floweth fuller every day,
> Perfect, yet it groweth deeper all the way.
>
> *Stayed upon Jehovah, hearts are fully blest*
> *Finding, as he promised, perfect peace and rest.*[1]

## Reflect on these points

1. *Most people do not experience peace because the threats they face are larger than the gods they serve. Do you agree? Why?*

2. *See if you can articulate the necessity of God's spiritual pattern: the preeminence of God, then the presence of God, and only then the peace of God.*

3. *What is the necessary connection between peace with God and the peace of God? Explain the differences. Expound upon their inter-relationship.*

4. *Why do you suppose God chose the metaphor of a river to speak of the life and peace he offers us?*

# Endnotes

## Preface

**1**  Woody Allen, *Side Effects* (New York: Ballantine Books, 1981), p. 81.

## Ch. 1  The preeminence of God

**1**  A. W. Tozer, *Knowledge of the Holy* (San Francisco: Harper and Row, 1961), p. 1.

**2**  We do not count the chapter and verse divisions of the Bible to be inspired as the text of Scripture is, but the divisions do highlight the structure of the book of Isaiah and its similarity to the whole of the Scriptures.

**3**  J. Elder Cumming, *Keswick Week 1906* (London: Marshalls, 1906), p. 22.

## Ch. 2  The preeminence of God over all the earth

**1**  "Weight of the Earth Hints at Big G," May 3, 2000, at: abc.net.au.

## Ch. 4  The preeminence of God over all idols

**1**  Francis Brown, S. R. Driver, and Charles A. Briggs, *A Hebrew and English Lexicon of the Old Testament* (Oxford: Clarendon Press, n.d.), p. 103.

**2**  Tozer, *Knowledge of the Holy*, pp. 3–4.

**3**  William Cowper, "O for a Closer Walk with God," 1772.

## Ch. 5  The preeminence of God over all the rulers

**1**  Cited in Edythe Draper, *Draper's Quotations for the Christian World* (Wheaton, IL: Tyndale House, 1992), p. 515.

**2**  Brown, Driver, and Briggs, *Hebrew and English Lexicon*, p. 931.

**3**  Ibid., p. 1047.

**4**  Isaiah 41:4; 42:8; 43:3, 10–13, 15, 25; 44:6, 8, 24–28; 45:5–6, 14, 18, 21–23; 46:9.

## Ch. 6  The preeminence of God over all the heavens

**1**  The title "the Holy One" is used by Isaiah more than any other writer of Scripture. His use of "Holy One" as a name for God is a strong argument in favor of a unified book of

Isaiah written by a single author (the name appears fourteen times in Isaiah 1–39 and fifteen times in Isaiah 40–66).

**2** Bill Bryson, *A Short History of Nearly Everything* (New York: Broadway Books, 2003), p. 18.

**3** Ibid., p. 33.

**4** Ibid., p.129.

**5** See "How Many Stars Are There in the Universe?", European Space Agency, February 23, 2004, at: www.esa.int.

**6** Ibid., pp. 24, 27.

**7** "Bush to Families: 'Entire Nation Grieves with You,'" February 1, 2003, at: www.cnn.com.

**8** Evelyn Husband and Donna VanLiere, *High Calling* (Nashville: Thomas Nelson, 2003), p. 159. Words of "God of Wonders" by Marc Byrd and Steve Hindalong, © 2000 New Spring Publishing, Inc. / Never Say Never Songs (ASCAP) (Administered by Brentwood-Benson Music Publishing, Inc.) / Storm Boy Music (BMI) / Meaux Mercy (BMI) (Admin. EMI Christian Music Group). All Rights Reserved. Used By Permission.

## Ch. 7  The presence of God

**1** A. W. Tozer, *The Pursuit of God* (Harrisburg, PA: Christian Publications, 1982), p. 64.

**2** Walter C. Kaiser, Jr., and R. Laird Harris, (ed.), "yāshab," in *Theological Wordbook of the Old Testament*, vol. i (Chicago: Moody Press, 1980), pp. 411–412.

**3** H. C. Leupold, *Exposition of the Psalms* (Grand Rapids, MI: Baker, 1969), p. 198.

**4** Tozer, *The Pursuit of God*, p. 71.

## Ch. 8  The presence of God is our comfort

**1** Marvin R. Wilson, and R. Laird Harris, (ed.), "naham," in *Theological Wordbook of the Old Testament* (Chicago: Moody Press, 1980), 2:570.

**2** Isa. 40:18, 25; 42:8; 43:11, 15; 44:6; 45:5–6, 14, 18, 21–22; 46:9; 47:10; 48:11.

**3** Isa. 41:8–9; 42:1, 19; 43:10; 44:1–2, 21; 45:4; 49:3, 5–6.

**4** J. Alec Motyer, *Isaiah: An Introduction and Commentary* (Downers Grove, IL: InterVarsity Press, 1999), p. 243; D. Martyn Lloyd-Jones, *The All-Sufficient God: Sermons on Isaiah 40* (Carlisle, PA: Banner of Truth, 2005).

## Ch. 9  The presence of God is our goal

**1** Ezek. 8:4; 9:3; 10:4, 18–19; 11:23.

**2** Matt. 3:3; Mark 1:2–3; Luke 3:4–6; John 1:23.

**3** Lloyd-Jones, *The All-Sufficient God*, p. 42.

## Ch. 11 The presence of God is our hope

**1** Matthew Henry, *Matthew Henry's Commentary on the Whole Bible: Complete and Unabridged in One Volume* (Peabody, MA: Hendriksen, 1991), p. 1152.

**2** Brown, Driver, and Briggs, *Hebrew and English Lexicon*, p. 1048.

**3** Marva J. Dawn, *To Walk and Not Faint: A Month of Meditations on Isaiah 40* (2nd edn.; Grand Rapids, MI: Eerdmans, 1997), p. 166.

**4** A. W. Tozer, *The Attributes of God: A Journey into the Father's Heart* (Camp Hill, PA: Christian Publications, 1997), p. 23.

## Ch. 12 The presence of God is our strength

**1** Brown, Driver, and Briggs, *Hebrew and English Lexicon*, p. 876.

**2** Ibid., p. 322.

## Ch. 13 The peace of God

**1** Frances R. Havergal, "Like a River Glorious," 1876.

# Also available

## Hints and signs of the coming King

Pictures of Jesus in the Old Testament

KURT STRASSNER

112PP, PAPERBACK

ISBN978-1-84625-208-2

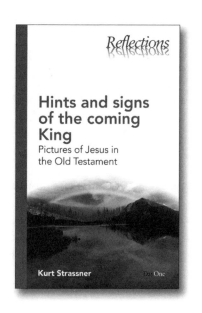

In the Bible, God often paints spiritual concepts with the bright colors of illustration: "Behold, the Lamb of God who takes away the sin of the world" (John 1:29). But it is not just Bible teaching that can be metaphoric; Bible events can be, too. God often worked out Bible history—real events, objects, and people—to show portraits of the greatest of all subjects—his beloved Son. This book examines eight such Old Testament pictures and demonstrates how they point us forward to Jesus Christ, the coming King.

'This book is an excellent evangelistic tool, particularly because it allows the eyes of our understanding to see Jesus through a number of "pictures" in the Old Testament. Whereas the Western world majors in abstract thought, I expect this book to find special appeal with us here in Africa where picture language is the way of communication. This book should be put into the hands of those who need to hear the gospel afresh in this simple picture form. I cannot commend it too highly!'
**CONRAD MBEWE, PASTOR OF KABWATA BAPTIST CHURCH, LUSAKA, ZAMBIA**

'Kurt Strassner's *Hints and Signs of the Coming King* provides an attractive guidebook to help us discover for ourselves how the Old Testament points to Jesus. What's more, you can read it, enjoy it, and learn life-long principles for your own Bible study—all in about the same length of time as a walk from Jerusalem to Emmaus. Enjoy the journey!'
**SINCLAIR B FERGUSON, SENIOR MINISTER, FIRST PRESBYTERIAN CHURCH, COLUMBIA, SOUTH CAROLINA**

# When God makes streams in the desert

Revival blessings in the Bible

ROGER ELLSWORTH

128PP, PAPERBACK

ISBN 978-1-84625-176-4

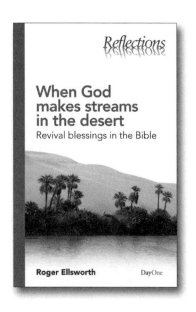

What is biblical revival? Many Christians associate revival with special meetings that used to take place once or twice a year. Guest preachers and singers would be brought in, and special evening services were designed to encourage believers to get closer to the Lord and to convince unbelievers to accept him as their Saviour.

But that is not revival. Biblical revival is about God bringing his people back to spiritual vitality. Only Christians can be revived because only they have spiritual life, having been regenerated by the Spirit of God on the basis of the redeeming work of Christ.

Learn what the Bible teaches about revival, and be inspired to pray that, even in our day, God will make streams flow in the desert!

'With a relentless focus on the Bible itself, Roger Ellsworth reminds us that true revival is a sovereign work of God that radically affects our lives. The best recommendation I can give of this book is that it made me long more intensely and pray more fervently for God to act in the midst of his people.'
**CHAD DAVIS, PASTOR, GRACE COMMUNITY CHURCH, MARTIN, TENNESSEE, USA**

'When God Makes Streams in the Desert reminds us that revival is present when, as Brian Edwards says, 'remarkable life and power that cannot be explained adequately in any human terms' moves into our churches and causes us to do what we do 'at a different level'. This book will change the way you think about and pray for revival.'
**PAUL ORRICK, PASTOR, FIRST BAPTIST CHURCH, GREENVILLE, OHIO, USA**

# On wings of prayer

Praying the ACTS way

REGGIE WEEMS

112PP, PAPERBACK

ISBN 978-1-84625-178-8

Constructing a prayer life is often like putting a puzzle together without the box's cover. Having a picture makes all the difference. Bible prayers create a model of what prayer can be; exciting, fulfilling and powerful. Using a simple acrostic makes prayer memorable, interesting and focused. You too can learn to pray following this simple outline utilized by men and women who experience the transforming power of prayer.

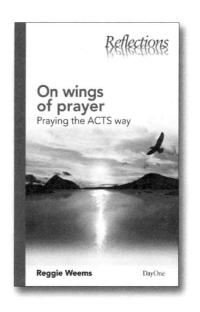

'This brief work on prayer will encourage you to pray, teach you to pray, and give you precious gems about prayer along the way. It taught me things I did not know, and reminded me of things I had forgotten.'
**PAUL DAVID WASHER, HEARTCRY MISSIONARY SOCIETY**

'Because of the unique nature of the Christian discipline of prayer, most books on prayer are more inspiring than they are helpful. Pastor Reggie Weems has achieved what only a few have ever done in Christian history. This book is orthodox, penetrating, motivating and inspiring, all in one slender, readable volume. If you are hoping to enhance your walk with the Master, here is one book that will bless your soul.'
**PAIGE PATTERSON, PRESIDENT, SOUTHWESTERN BAPTIST THEOLOGICAL SEMINARY, FORT WORTH, TEXAS, USA**

# They echoed the voice of God

Reflections on the Minor Prophets

ROGER ELLSWORTH

128PP, PAPERBACK

ISBN 978-1-84625-101-6

Many carry a little Bible and believe in a little God. Their Bibles are little because they ignore so many of its books. Their God is little because they ignore so many of the Bible's truths. The Minor Prophets can help us. These men made sense of their circumstances and found strength for their challenges by basking in the God who was above it all and in it all. The God they served was wise enough to plan and strong enough to achieve. This study of their messages will help us have both bigger Bibles and a bigger God.

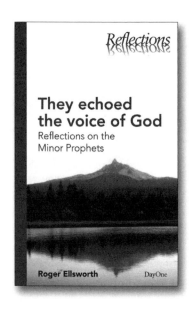

'Roger Ellsworth helps us appreciate how the so-called Minor Prophets make known the character and work of our great God. This book is a great introduction to and overview of their prophecies. Read it to become acquainted with these sometimes overlooked servants and, more importantly, with the unchangeable God whose message they proclaimed.'
**Tom Ascol, Director of Founders Ministries and Pastor, Grace Baptist Church, Cape Coral, Florida**

'Laced with helpful, practical application, this book shows how each prophet emphasized a particular aspect of God's character, giving an overall picture that is compelling.'
**Jim Winter, Minister of Horsell Evangelical Church, Woking**

# About Day One:

Day One's threefold commitment:
- To be faithful to the Bible, God's inerrant, infallible Word;
- To be relevant to our modern generation;
- To be excellent in our publication standards.

*I continue to be thankful for the publications of Day One. They are biblical; they have sound theology; and they are relevant to the issues at hand. The material is condensed and manageable while, at the same time, being complete—a challenging balance to find. We are happy in our ministry to make use of these excellent publications.*

**JOHN MACARTHUR, PASTOR-TEACHER, GRACE COMMUNITY CHURCH, CALIFORNIA**

*It is a great encouragement to see Day One making such excellent progress. Their publications are always biblical, accessible and attractively produced, with no compromise on quality. Long may their progress continue and increase!*

**JOHN BLANCHARD, AUTHOR, EVANGELIST AND APOLOGIST**

Visit our web site for more information and
to request a free catalogue of our books.

www.dayone.co.uk